Stonewall Jackson Day By Day

D1561966

By
John W. Schildt

John W. Schildt

i

With thanks for the beauty of the Shenandoah Valley, and for the mystical moments I have experienced in tracing JACKSON DAY BY DAY.

TYPOGRAPHY AND COMPOSITION
The News-Gazette
Lexington, Virginia

DIRECTOR OF PRODUCTION James Dedrick
PRODUCTION ASSOCIATES Cheryl Garrett,
Ree Breeden, Shirley Ziegler, Anita Emore
Walter Lunsford, Matthew W. Paxton, IV

What? Another book about Jackson? Hasn't everything possible been said about him? Not quite. He has had his splendid biographers in Col. G.F.R. Henderson, Dr. Frank Vandiver, and others. His tactics have been told and retold by Dr. Douglas Southall Freeman, Robert G. Tanner, and other writers about the Civil War. Personal accounts have been shared by Henry Kyd Douglas and Alexander Swift Pendleton.

Now from the OFFICIAL RECORDS, Jackson's personal letters, papers, and writings of Jed Hotchkiss and James Power Smith, also staff members, we present a day by day account of the military career of the man they called "STONEWALL," telling where he was and what he did. Or in other words, JACKSON DAY BY DAY.

John W. Schildt
Chewsville, Maryland
16 December 1980

With Gratitude

The idea for this book came after a delightful tour of Jackson's Valley Campaign with the Chicago Civil War Round Table in May of 1980. They sparked the interest.

My thanks is also given to John Divine of Waterford, Virginia, for fatherly advice and the loan of books.

Robert Krick, Chief Historian at Fredericksburg supplied information on General Gregg, Moss Neck, and Yerby's. Chris Calkins gave aid at the Jackson shrine. The Park Service can be proud of two outstanding gentlemen and scholars.

Mrs. Julia S. Martin of the Information Office at the Virginia Military Institute went above the call of duty in answering questions and letters.

And Lowell Reidenbaugh, Editor of the "Sporting News," a devoted Jackson scholar supplied leads and notes from his library.

CONTENTS

ILLUSTRATIONS

I

THE MAN

It was June 23, 1897. The place, the Virginia Military Institute[1] in Lexington, Virginia. The occasion, the dedication of the Jackson Memorial Hall. The speaker was Dr. Hunter Holmes McGuire[2] of Richmond, formerly the surgeon of the famed Stonewall Brigade, and the doctor of Thomas Jonathan Jackson, an obscure professor at V.M.I. who rose to fame and immortality in the Civil War.

McGuire was quite an orator. He compared his friend Jackson to King Arthur, Alexander the Great, and King Constantine. Dr. McGuire noted that in the past two hundred years, the English speaking world had produced five great soldiers, and three of them were Virginians. He listed the great generals as Marlborough, Washington, Wellington, Lee and Jackson. He said that Jackson's Valley Campaign was superior to those of Napolean.

Dr. McGuire may have exaggerated just a bit. However, thousands have praised the man they called "Stonewall." His name is known throughout the military world. And many great military leaders have studied his philosophy and tactics. A lot of them have used his campaigns as a model. Certainly Thomas Jonathan Jackson, ranks as one of the great military figures of all time. But what manner of man was he?

Jackson was born in Clarksburg, Virginia, now West Virginia, on January 21, 1824. He was left an orphan at an early age, and apparently was cared for by several uncles who treated him like a nephew.[3] Little is known of his childhood. However, he did not like to lose at anything. As a boy he showed a lot of spunk, and never feared fighting someone bigger and stronger.

Like most other children of his day, Tom went to school part time, and worked the rest either on the uncle's farm or at the family mill. He was quiet and studied a lot. Tom could always be depended on. Promptness and attention to the clock were of the utmost importance.

There must have been many grins and much amusement when Jackson arrived at West Point. He looked like something "straight from the hills." Dressed in homespun, and carrying his belongings in a pair of old saddlebags, he looked like "a hick."

He had difficulty with math, but studied hard, and steadily rose in class standing. Being aloof and reserved, he received some criticism for being unfriendly. Others, though, admired his efforts.

Tom graduated in 1846,[4] and was assigned to the First U.S. Artillery. He welcomed the chance to serve in the Mexican War[5] and did so with distinction and bravery. After some routine assignments, he resigned from the army to become a professor at the Virginia Military Institute in Lexington.

Jackson did not set the academic world on fire. He was not a good teacher. Students slept in his class, and made fun of him. They had all kinds of nicknames for him and none complimentary.

While in Lexington, Jackson met Elinor Junkin, the daughter of Dr. George Junkin,[6] the President of Washington College. They were married on August 4, 1853. Jackson was grief stricken when she died fourteen months later. He then married Mary Anna Morrison,[7] the daughter of a Presbyterian minister on July 16, 1857. The wedding took place at Cottage Home, North Carolina. They went to Saratoga, West Point and Niagara Falls on their honeymoon.

The North and South were drifting apart, and the flames that were being fanned, burst into the open on the night of October 16, 1859. That evening, John Brown led a raid on Harpers Ferry. Col. Robert E. Lee and Lt. James E.B. Stuart were sent to the Ferry to capture Brown and put an end to the situation. The South looked upon his raid as an invasion, while the North looked upon Brown as a hero.

Brown was sentenced to be hanged. This caused a great outcry in the North, and Jackson along with 85 VMI cadets were among those sent to keep peace at the hanging on December 2, 1859.

Tom did not approve of secession. He hoped the Civil War could be averted. Yet he firmly believed in States Rights and placed the State above the nation. Had the war not come, his career "would probably been that of a college professor of mediocre teaching ability."

Jackson has had many great biographers. And it is not the intention of this book to go into detail about his life, other than the daily events of his military career. Perhaps a few lines from others will tell us about the manner of man he was.

Jackson was reserved and silent, a good listener who grasped detail. D.H. Hill[8] says he was a nervous individual. He was deeply religious, and a man of prayer, hesitating to fight on Sunday. He believed that no man or cause could succeed without the favor of God. He was modest, and attributed his success to God. "The Richmond Examiner" said "there was the stuff of Cromwell in Jackson. Hannibal might have been proud of his campaign in the Valley."

Dabney[9] talked about his great courage, and devotion to detail. His appearance and manner lacked that which draws men. He was no MacArther, Patton, or McClellan in appearance. He was tough, cold and strict, but his soldiers worshipped him. "Jackson was a surprise, nobody understood him." Yet next to Robert E. Lee he was the most loved man in the army, and commanded the respect and admiration of his foes."

Thomas Jonathan Jackson

(Courtesy, The Library of Congress)

II
SPARKS

On November 6, 1860, Abraham Lincoln was elected President of the United States. The South had great doubts about the Republicans and about the man who was to occupy the White House. They felt threatened.

Therefore, on December 18, leaders of South Carolina met at Charleston. In a carnival-like atmosphere, they dissolved the ratification of the U.S. Constitution and seceded from the Union. The people of the South were shocked by this action. However, South Carolina was soon joined by Mississippi, Florida, Alabama, Georgia, Louisiana and Texas.[1]

Delegates from these states met at Montgomery, Alabama on February 4, to form a provisional government for the Confederate States of America. Five days later, Jefferson Davis was chosen as the President. Thus a divided nation faced Mr. Lincoln.

When the southern states seceded, they seized nearly all Federal installations and property within their boundaries. The day after his inauguration, Mr. Lincoln received shocking news. Fort Sumter was low on food and other provisions. The commander, Major Robert Anderson, felt only a show of force would cause South Carolina to permit a relief shipment.

However, Lincoln did not want a confrontation. Should he evacuate the fort or try to send supplies? In an effort to maintain peace, he sent his friend Ward Hill Lamon to talk with the Governor of South Carolina. But the situation was hopeless. There was to be no negotations. Jefferson Davis and the Confederate cabinet met and demanded the surrender of the fort. General P.G.T. Beauregard was to be in charge of the operation. Major Anderson refused to surrender. And at 4:30 a.m., on April 12, the first shot of the Civil War was fired.

The war was on. Four days later, Mr. Lincoln called for 75,000 men to put down the rebellion. North Carolina, Arkansas and Tennessee joined the Confederate ranks.

The Commonwealth of Virginia held out as long as possible. But with her sister states joining the Southern ranks, the shots fired on Fort Sumter and the call for soldiers to suppress the South, Virginia had to make a choice. The Old Dominion "had to take her stand with her Southern sisters."

A few days after Fort Sumter, April 18, Virginia militia dashed into Harpers Ferry, the gateway of the Shenandoah Valley in an effort to prevent the destruction of the U.S. Arsenal. The town where

John Brown had caused so much trouble was now in the hands of the State of Virginia.[2]

The previous day, a secret session of the Virginia legislature voted to secede by a vote of 81 to 51. The decision was kept quiet until Virginia troops could reach Harpers Ferry. The supplies were needed. When the news of secession reached the Shenandoah Valley,[3] there was great joy, although many realized there would be a long hard struggle with many tears and much suffering.

On April 27, Colonel Robert E. Lee, the man who had declined the command of the Army of the United States and the officer now in charge of all Virginia forces ordered an officer and professor from Virginia Military Institute in Lexington to take command of all the forces at Harpers Ferry. With this order we begin the story of JACKSON - DAY BY DAY.[4]

During the period covering just a little more than two years, Jackson was in these locations:

April 29 - June 15, 1861, the Harpers Ferry area;

June 16 - July 18, Falling Waters, Bunker Hill, Winchester;

July 19 - Nov. 4, Manassas and Centreville;

Nov. 5 - March 11, 1862 Winchester and Romney Expedition;

March 12 - June 12, the famous Valley Campaign;

June 17 - July 14, the Peninsula and defenses of Richmond;

August 1862, the Gordonsville area, Cedar Mountain, and Second Manassas;

September 4 - Sept. 18, Western Maryland, Harpers Ferry, and Antietam;

September 19 - Nov. 22, the panhandle of what is now West Virginia and Winchester;

December 1, 1862 - April 29, 1863, Fredericksburg, Moss Neck and Yerby's;

May 1 - 3, 1863, Chancellorsville Campaign.

Saturday, April 20, 1861. This evening orders came from the Governor's office in Richmond for the Virginia Military Institute Cadets to come to the capital city. Jackson, as the senior officer present on campus, was to be in command.

The Virginia Military Institute, Lexington, Virginia

(Courtesy V.M.I.)

Sunday, April 21, 1861. Jackson was so excited he missed breakfast. He asked Dr. White[5] to have prayer with the cadets before they left. At 11:00 a.m. he came home and went with Anna to the bedroom. There they read from the Holy Scriptures, "For we know that if our earthly house of this tabernacle be dissolved, we have a building of God, a house not made with hands eternal in the heavens." Tom's voice was choked with emotion as he and his wife knelt in prayer, and as the husband he committed them both to God's care.[6]

The Cadets were to march at 12:30. The command was formed. Dr. White offered prayer and then they waited. At precisely 12:30 p.m., Jackson gave the order to march. They proceeded to stagecoaches which took them to Staunton and the trains. Jackson left his beloved Lexington for the last time. It took a while to make the thirty-mile trip via horse drawn equipment. So Jackson's first night in the military in the Civil War was spent at Staunton.

Monday, April 22, 1861. Jackson and the cadets from VMI left Staunton late in the morning. An engine derailed in passing through a tunnel in the Blue Ridge Mountains. This caused a delay of two hours. In the midst of repairs, Jackson wrote to his wife.[7]

Traveling through the small Virginia towns, the lads from the West Point of the South were hailed with cheers. The weather was great. And war seemed romantic. The train reached Richmond at night and the soldiers were marched off to the fairgrounds to make camp. Jackson had delivered the cadets so he was temporarily out of work.

Tuesday, April 23, 1861. News reached Richmond and Jackson that Robert E. Lee had resigned from the U.S. Army and was coming home to take command of the Virginia forces. Jackson felt Lee was the best man available.

Wednesday, April 24, 1861. While waiting for an assignment, Jackson helped with duties at Camp Instruction, now renamed Camp Lee.

Thursday, April 25, 1861. Jackson received an appointment today as major of engineers. This disturbed him greatly. He hated engineering. The rank was an insult. He was a West Point graduate, a combat veteran, and a military instructor and was seeing men with political pull and no experience being made colonels. Worse yet was the fact that he was given a desk job.

This was a terrible fate for a man who had the military drive of a Patton.

Friday, April 26, 1861. News of Jackson's treatment reached an old friend, Jonathan M. Bennett who immediately called on Governor Letcher. "Such an assignment is a waste," said Bennett. The Governor was impressed, and Jackson was made a Colonel. Call it Providence or whatever, but perhaps Jackson and history owe Bennett a great debt of thanks for giving him the opportunity to shine.

Saturday, April 27, 1861. This morning Jackson was given his commission as a Colonel in the Virginia State forces. Gov. Letcher asked him to go to Harpers Ferry, the location of the U.S. Arsenal and a gateway to the Shenandoah Valley. Jackson was to take command of the raw militia, construct some type of defense and await orders from General Lee.

Sunday, April 28, 1861. Jackson started his second trip of the war on Sunday. Last week he left Lexington. Now he was leaving, "for the post I prefer above all others...Don't expect to hear from me very often...Don't be concerned about your husband, for our kind Heavenly Father will give every needful aid."[8]

The trip was rough, going by way of Gordonsville, to Manassas Junction, then west to Strasburg in the Valley. From Strasburg to Winchester, Jackson traveled by horse, arriving late at night. The trip caused Jackson to write to Richmond urging the construction of a military railroad.

Monday, April 29, 1861. Tom Jackson made the last leg of his trip from Winchester to Harpers Ferry by train. He and Major J.T.L. Preston[9] took rooms in a small hotel near the railroad bridge.

Tuesday, April 30, 1861. Jackson published an order saying he was in command. The militia officers did not like this. There was strong independent feeling in the ranks and little love for outsiders, regardless of their credentials. Jackson had to determine how many men were present for duty, and the condition of camps, food, supplies, etc.

This month was spent at Harpers Ferry. The first three weeks were devoted to making soldiers out of the raw recruits and instilling discipline.

John B. Imboden from Staunton was one of the first Virginians to arrive when Governor Letcher sent state troops to take over the Ferry. In late April, Imboden was sent back to Richmond in an effort to obtain munitions and supplies.

On the 10th, Robert E. Lee was named commander of all Virginia troops, and all militia officers above the rank of captain lost their standing. Naturally this caused a lot of trouble for Jackson.

But when Imboden arrived back in Harpers Ferry in mid May, he was amazed at the change. The militia officers were gone. And he found Jackson and his adjutant in a "little wayside hotel near the railroad bridge." Imboden requested and got an interview and delivered papers from Lee.

> Jackson and his adjutant were at a little pine table figuring upon the troops present. They were dressed in well-worn, dingy uniforms of professors in the Virginia Military Institute...[10]

Imboden later returned to his Staunton battery and told them they were required to muster into service, "either for twelve months or during the war." He urged them to sign up for the duration. To this they shouted, "For the war! For the war!" The mustering ceremony was held, and Imboden poudly took the roll to Jackson. He was happy and replied, "Thank you, captain - thank you; and please thank your men for me." This was the first unit to be mustered.

Imboden offers a great description of Jackson as he found him in May of 1861.

> The presence of a master mind was visible in the changed condition of the camp. Perfect order reigned everywhere. Instruction in the details of military duties occupied Jackson's whole time. He urged the officers to call upon him for information about even the minutest details of duty...He was a rigid disciplinarian, and yet as gentle and kind as a woman. He was the easiest man in our army to get along with pleasantly so long as one did his duty...[11]

We dwell on this because it shows "what manner of man he was," and also because these were the days when he shaped the unit later to be known as the Stonewall Brigade.

Wednesday, May 1, 1861. At Harpers Ferry.

Thursday, May 2, 1861. At Harpers Ferry

Friday, May 3, 1861. At Harpers Ferry

Saturday, May 4, 1861. At Harpers Ferry

Sunday, May 5, 1861. At Harpers Ferry

Monday, May 6, 1861. At Harpers Ferry

Tuesday, May 7, 1861. At Harpers Ferry

Wednesday, May 8, 1861. By this time Jackson was living in a very nice house in Harpers Ferry, apparently the home of the former Supt. of the U.S. Armory, Mr. Barbour. Col. Preston was with him.[12]

Thursday, May 9, 1861. At Harpers Ferry.

Friday, May 10, 1861. Harpers Ferry. Robert E. Lee assumes command of all Virginia forces.

Saturday, May 11, 1861. At Harpers Ferry

Sunday, May 12, 1861. On this day, or close to it, Jackson spotted a horse he liked on some captured Baltimore and Ohio stock. It was a small sorrel and would make a good present for his wife. Being an honest man, he paid the quartermaster. However, Jackson became so fond of the horse that he kept it and the horse became famous as Jackson's "Little Sorrel." It's remains were mounted and can be seen in the VMI Museum.

Monday, May 13, 1861. At Harpers Ferry.

Tuesday, May 14, 1861. At Harpers Ferry.

Wednesday, May 15, 1861. Harpers Ferry. Senator James Mason of Virginia writes of Jackson, "I spent the evening and night at Colonel Jackson's headquarters, and even my limited observations there confirmed the general tone of all around him, that all were in good hands under his command."

Thursday, May 16, 1861. At Harpers Ferry.

Friday, May 17, 1861. At Harpers Ferry.

Saturday, May 18, 1861. At Harpers Ferry.

Sunday, May 19, 1861. At Harpers Ferry. Jackson rides south to Point of Rocks to visit John Imboden in charge of the outpost there. Some of the guards thought Jackson and his friend were spies. Jackson told Imboden not to tell the others who he was, but that he was pleased with things at Point of Rocks.

Monday, May 20, 1861. At Harpers Ferry.

Tuesday, May 21, 1861. At Harpers Ferry. Leaders in Richmond were growing very concerned about feelings in northwestern Virginia. Jackson had some thoughts which he conveyed to Lee.

> I would suggest that a force destined for the northwest be assembled, ostensibly for the defense of this part of the State, at Winchester, or some point near here, and that the moment that the governor's proclamation announces the ratification by the people of the ordinance of secession, such troops be put in the cars, as though they were coming to this place, but that they be immediately thrown into the north-west, and at once crush out opposition...You will pardon me for urging promptness...Any want of this may be disastrous.[13]

Wednesday, May 22, 1861. At Harpers Ferry.

Thursday, May 23, 1861. At Harpers Ferry

Friday, May 24, 1861. At Harpers Ferry. Jackson had a surprise today. Brig. Gen. Joseph E. Johnston arrived to take command of Harpers Ferry. He had had a long and brilliant career in the regular army of the United States. Confederate leaders felt an officer beyond the mere rank of major should be in command at such an important post as Harpers Ferry. Johnston brought an engineering and quartermaster officer with him. Jackson read the letter from Lee, "Referred to General Joseph E. Johnston, commanding officer at Harpers Ferry. By order of Maj. Gen. Lee."

Jackson obeyed orders, but must have been a little stung. He felt he had performed his duties well. He had instilled discipline, lifted morale, established good campsites, and disrupted the B and O. Now he was being replaced. It was true that he had made some decisions on his own. But he was the officer on the spot, and at times could not wait for word from

Richmond.

For a few days Jackson would have little to do. However, this meant more time for reflection, and letters to Anna.

Saturday, May 25, 1861. At Harpers Ferry.

Sunday, May 26, 1861. At Harpers Ferry.

Monday, May 27, 1861. At Harpers Ferry.

Tuesday, May 28, 1861. At Harpers Ferry.

Wednesday, May 29, 1861. At Harpers Ferry.

Thursday, May 30, 1861. At Harpers Ferry.

Friday, May 31, 1861. At Harpers Ferry.

—————— Harpers Ferry ——————

Saturday, June 1, 1861. Shenandoah Valley units were entrusted to Jackson and designated the First Brigade. They were the Second, Fourth, Fifth and Twenty-seventh Virginia Infantry Regiments, and the Rockbridge Artillery. This was to become one of America's greatest fighting units. The brigade has been compared to crack units of Alexander the Great, Caesar's Tenth Legion, and the Old Guard of Napoleon. Douglas S. Freeman termed it "The Southern Cromwell's Model Brigade."

Dr. James Robertson has done a tremendous study on "THE STONEWALL BRIGADE."[14] So we just look briefly at the regiments Jackson welded into a crack combat team. They were young men, and most came from the Shenandoah Valley of Virginia.

Forty-nine rifle companies comprised the five regiments of infantry designated as the First Brigade. The Second Regiment came largely from the Winchester, Charles Town, Berryville area. Many of the men in the Thirty-Third Regiment came from the same region, as well as Harrisonburg. The Fourth Regiment came primarily from the southern end of the Shenandoah Valley. Staunton and Augusta County provided the manpower for the Fifth, and Lexington furnished the nucleus for the Twenty-seventh.

Sunday, June 2, 1861. Harpers Ferry.

Monday, June 3, 1861. Harpers Ferry.

Tuesday, June 4, 1861. Jackson wrote to his wife, and talked to her about the lack of news. Naturally, he said he could not be expected to tell her about military matters. Then he shared with her information in which women are interested. He told her "I have a nice, green yard, and if you were only here, how much we could enjoy it together...My chamber is on the second story, and the roses climb even to that height...I wish you could see with me the beautiful roses in the yard and garden, and upon the wall of the house...but my sweet, little sunny face is what I want to see most of all...I have been greatly blessed by our kind Heavenly Father, in health and otherwise, since leaving home..."[15]

Tom goes on to tell her the troops have been divided into brigades, and he has been named commander of the First Brigade.

Wednesday, June 5, 1861. At Harpers Ferry.

Thursday, June 6, 1861. At Harpers Ferry.

Friday, June 7, 1861. At Harpers Ferry.

Saturday, June 8, 1861. At Harpers Ferry.

Sunday, June 9, 1861. At Harpers Ferry.

Monday, June 10, 1861. At Harpers Ferry.

Tuesday, June 11, 1861. At Harpers Ferry. One evening during this period, Jackson announced to the troops that Hunter Holmes McGuire had been appointed Brigade Surgeon. McGuire, of nearby Winchester had arrived at the Ferry with the 2nd Virginia. Jackson thought he was too young and inexperienced to be a physician. Therefore, he had McGuire investigated, and when he found he was capable, he announced his appointment to the troops. This was the first inkling McGuire had of the appointment.[16]

Wednesday, June 12, 1861. At Harpers Ferry.

Thursday, June 13, 1861. This morning, Jackson was given orders to get ready to evacuate Harpers Ferry. He expected to march out in the evening, but the order did not come.

Friday, June 14, 1861. Joe Johnston withdrew his forces from Maryland and Loudoun Heights. (And) "has blown up and burnt the railroad bridge across the Potomac and is doing the same with respect to the public buildings. Today, Alexander Swift "Sandie" Pendleton reported for duty at Harpers Ferry. There was no real need for an engineering officer so Sandie drilled with the Rockbridge Artillery commanded by his father. Soon he would report to Jackson.[17]

Saturday, June 15, 1861. Final preparations made for evacation from Harpers Ferry. Henry Kyd Douglas had mixed feelings about blowing the Bridge at Shepherdstown. It was partly his father's, as his dad owned stock in the company.[18]

Sunday, June 16, 1861. Six weeks of duty at Harpers Ferry came to an end today. "By order of General Johnston, the entire force left Harpers Ferry, marched through Charlestown, and halted for the night about two miles this side."

Jackson had shown rapid growth and development at the Ferry. His hard work was about ready to produce great dividends, and eventual fame. In fact, his troops marched at the rate of three miles an hour. Jackson had great hopes, "I trust that through the blessing of God we shall soon be given an opportunity of driving the invaders from this region."[19]

Monday, June 17, 1861. Today, "we moved toward the enemy, who were between Martinsburg and Williamsport, Maryland, and encamped for the night at Bunker Hill. "This would be the first of many nights in the Bunker Hill area over the next eighteen months. Jackson had hoped to be the aggressor and march to attack the Union forces. Instead, Johnston proposed a defensive position, and the command did not move until noon. Therefore, camp was not made until sunset.

Tuesday, June 18, 1861. At Harpers Ferry.

Wednesday, June 19, 1861. Johnston ordered Jackson to Martinsburg to do as much damage as possible to the Baltimore and Ohio Railroad Depot. Four locomotives were sent back to Winchester, drawn by teams of horses.

Thursday, June 20, 1861. The work of wrecking things in Martinsburg continued. There appeared a prospect for battle, but Union forces retreated before the Confederate advance. "Our troops are very anxious for an engagement..." Jackson learned that more Union troops were crossing the Potomac at Williamsport. The next week was spent in the task of disrupting the railroad.

Harpers Ferry, Jackson's first Civil War command.
The destruction of the bridge.

Friday, June 21, 1861. In the Martinsburg area.

Saturday, June 22, 1861. The First Virginia Brigade was encamped today about four miles north of Martinsburg. They called their bivouac area, Camp Stevens.[20]

Sunday, June 23, 1861. North of Martinsburg.

Monday, June 24, 1861. Jackson advanced with Allen's regiment of infantry, and the Rockbridge Artillery, but once again Union forces recrossed the Potomac River to the Maryland shore. Jackson examined their camps, there were two of them, and estimated they had 900 men. Once again he expressed the desire for action. Jackson was convinced "that the enemy is afraid to meet us." A.S. Pendleton was named ordnance officer for the brigade. He and Jackson became very close, almost like father and son.

Tuesday, June 25, 1861. North of Martinsburg.

Wednesday, June 26, 1861. North of Martinsburg, close to the Potomac. Near Williamsport, one of his men was shot in the abdomen by a disloyal person.

Thursday, June 27, 1861. Jackson wrote to his wife saying he was sleeping outdoors with no covering. The General did not like the disloyalty in Berkeley County. He discussed this with Ned Lee, Rev. Pendleton's son-in-law who was from Shepherdstown.[21]

Friday, June 28, 1861. North of Martinsburg, on scouting and patrol.

Saturday, June 29, 1861. At Camp Stevens, north of Martinsburg.

Sunday, June 30, 1861. At Camp Stevens.

Monday, July 1, 1861. At Camp Stevens.

Tuesday, July 2, 1861. Falling Waters, Virginia. About 4:00 a.m., General Robert Patterson crossed the Potomac from Williamsport, Maryland and headed south. Three-fourth of the 14,000 men were on the main road to Martinsburg. They wanted to clear the area of Confederates.
About 7:30 a.m. Col. Jackson, bivouaced at Camp Stevens, received word from James Ewell Brown Stuart about the

Jackson Day By Day

Union crossing and advance. Jackson ordered Kenton's regiment and Pendleton's Battery forward. The blue and the gray met near Hoke's Run. This was Jackson's first action of the war, his baptism of fire. The Confederates fought from the Porterfield farm. The barn was destroyed.

According to some sources, Captain Pendleton who had named his guns, "Matthew, Mark, Luke, and John," gave an order, to "Aim, Fire Low, and may God have mercy on their souls."

After a brisk skirmish, realizing the superior number of his opponent, and fearing a flank movement, or the possibility of Stuart being cut off, Jackson gave the order to "fall back."

Patterson occupied Camp Stevens, and made his headquarters in Martinsburg. Jackson camped at Big Spring. Joseph E. Johnston, Commander of the Army of the Shenandoah, was so pleased with the actions of Stuart and Jackson, that he recommended their immediate promotion, saying:

> Each of these two officers has, since the commencement of hostilities, been exercising the command corresponding to the next grade above the commission he holds, and proved himself fully competent to such command. I, therefore, respectfully recommend that Colonel Jackson be promoted without delay to the grade of Brigadier General...[22]

Twelve Confederates were wounded, and thirteen killed or missing.

Jackson felt his men "behaved beautifully."[23]

Wednesday, July 3, 1861. At Darksville, not far from Martinsburg. The Confederates hoped to lure Patterson into battle. But the fight did not come.

Thursday, July 4, 1861. At Darksville. This morning one of Johnston's staff officers told Jackson he had been recommended for brigadier-general. Tom wrote to Anna saying, "I am very thankful that an ever-kind Providence made me an instrument in carrying out General Johnston's orders so successfully...The enemy are celebrating the 4th of July in Martinsburg, but we are not observing the day."[24]

Part of the Yankee celebration caused tragedy. Seventeen-year-old Belle Boyd shot and killed a Union soldier at her home in South Queen Street in Martinsburg. He had entered her home and was searching it. The family was distressed because the Yankees wanted to tear down the Confederate flags in the various rooms, and fly the Union flag over the house.

Friday, July 5, 1861. At Darksville.

Saturday, July 6, 1861. At Darksville.

Sunday, July 7, 1861. At Darksville.

Monday, July 8, 1861. Near Martinsburg.

Tuesday, July 9, 1861. Near Martinsburg.

Wednesday, July 10, 1861. Near Martinsburg.

Thursday, July 11, 1861. Near Martinsburg.

Friday, July 12, 1861. Near Martinsburg.

Saturday, July 13, 1861. Near Martinsburg.

Sunday, July 14, 1861. Near Martinsburg.

Monday, July 15, 1861. Winchester.

Tuesday, July 16, 1861. Winchester. The Yankees were only ten miles away now at Bunker Hill. Jackson was ready to give them a warm reception if they advanced, but they did not. The General was in good spirits, "God will, I am well satisfied, in His own good time and way, give us the victory..."

Keeping his wife abreast of what he was doing, Jackson notes "I am sleeping on the floor of a good room, but I have been sleeping out in camp several weeks, and generally found that it agreed with me, except when it rained...Sleeping in the open air, with no covering but my blankets and the blue sky for a canopy, is more refreshing than sleeping in a room." Cornbread was a main part of his diet. He stated that he still was not happy about mailing letters that would travel on the Sabbath. He was convinced that living according to Bible principles was the best policy to follow. "Look how our kind Heavenly Father has prospered us...I am in the path of duty, and no evil can come nigh me. All things work together for my good. "He begged his wife to send him long letters, "and when the wars and troubles are over, I trust that, through divine mercy, we shall have many happy days together."[25]

Wednesday, July 17, 1861. Winchester. This sojourn in Winchester was about over. Tomorrow he would strike his tents and head east.

Jackson Day By Day

III
"A STONEWALL"

Thursday, July 18, 1861. On the march from Winchester toward Manassas. "I struck my tents, rolled them up, and left them on the ground, and about noon marched through Winchester...About an hour and a half after leaving, I had the following order from General Johnston published to my brigade: 'Our gallant army under General Beauregard is now attacked by overwhelming numbers. The commanding general hopes that his troops will step out like men, and make a forced march to save the country.' At this stirring appeal the soldiers rent the air with shouts of joy..."[1] The march then continued until the column reached Millwood in Clarke County. There a halt was ordered for an hour. A good stream of water was found and the men ate.

Then the men plodded on, inspired by the memories of the day in Winchester, the cheers of the people, and regimental bands playing "Dixie," and "The Bonnie Blue Flag."[2] They reached the Shenandoah River about dark. It was waist deep, and it took a while for all the men to cross.

Friday, July 19, 1861. In the first few moments of this day, Jackson's men tramp through Ashby Gap. They are weary, having been marching since mid-afternoon. At 2:00 a.m. the commander calls a halt. The men fall asleep where they stop. Jackson himself stands guard, the event prompting the poem "The Lone Sentinel."[3] A marker near Paris, Virginia describes the event. After daybreak the troops reach the Manassas Gap Railroad and load freight cars and start the final leg of the journey toward Manassas. They are hurrying from the Valley to reinforce comrades threatened by the Union advance from Washington. Late in the day, they go into camp just behind Blackburn's and Mitchell's Ford.

Saturday, July 20, 1861. Preparing for action at Manassas.

Sunday, July 21, 1861. History often asks the question, "Do men make the events, or do the events of history make the man." Perhaps it's a combination of each. Today, the Battle of Manassas gave a man a chance, and the man responded. As a result, Thomas Jonathan Jackson won a reputation and nickname which lasts even today.

As the fighting raged back and forth, Jackson was called to reinforce other troops. His strict discipline and training paid off. Just as a coach drives a team so it can be a winner, so now Jackson's constant drilling paid dividends. In the midst of the action General Bee called out to his troops, "Look! There's Jackson standing like a stone wall! Rally behind the Virginians." The event gave a name in history to a man and troops he had whipped into a to flight combat unit.[4]

Jackson was shot in the finger during the action. This happened while waving his men on. One doctor wanted to take it off, but the General waited for Dr. McGuire's opinion, and the finger stayed on.

He performed well. Indeed he was flushed with the excitement of victory, and led cheers for President Davis.

"The summer months went by without further fighting on the Potomac." Ranks were depleted by furlough and by illness. Many of the soliders were bored with military routine, and upset by having to obey orders of a commander. The First Brigade fared pretty well. Many thought it was because Jackson moved the campsites, and insisted on life in the fresh air. He did not permit the men to loaf. There was constant drill and training. The men did not appreciate this, and grumbled as soldiers will, but Jackson was doing it to improve their ability as soldiers. Henderson covers this period in two pages. Vandiver records it on seven pages.

Monday, July 22, 1861. In camp near Manassas Junction.

Tuesday, July 23, 1861. In camp near Manassas Junction.

Wednesday, July 24, 1861. Near Manassas Junction.

Thursday, July 25, 1861. Near Manassas Junction.

Friday, July 26, 1861. Near Manassas Junction.

Saturday, July 27, 1861. Near Manassas Junction.

Sunday, July 28, 1861. Near Manassas Junction.

Monday, July 29, 1861. Near Manassas Junction.

Tuesday, July 30, 1861. Near Manassas Junction. Bivouac area called "Camp Maggot."

"There Stands Jackson Like a Stonewall, Rally Behind The Virginians." First Manassas, July 21, 1861.

Wednesday, July 31, 1861. Near Manassas Junction. Typhoid fever starts to hit camp.

Thursday August 1, 1861. Near Manassas Junction.

Friday, August 2, 1861. Today Jackson received permission to move camp one mile east of Centreville for health reasons. Troops were glad to move from the smell and sights of the battlefield.

This bivouac area was called Camp Harmon. Jackson and the First Brigade remained here until September 16, when they moved to a site near Fairfax Court House.

While at Camp Harmon, Mrs. Jackson came for a visit. The General, in company with General Pendleton, took her over the battlefield in an ambulance. Anna was amazed to find Bull Run such a small stream. She saw the Henry house riddled with shot and shell. She could hardly believe so many had fallen, and death had reaped such a harvest.

The Jacksons stayed at the Utterbach home. Anna ate with him at the staff table. Anna came back for a visit at Fairfax in late September. Otherwise, these are the hidden days of Jackson's career. From August to November, very little material is available.[5]

The last days of August were spent at Manassas Junction. The period August 2 - September 16 near Centreville, and the last seven weeks prior to leaving for Winchester, near Fairfax Court House. Headquarters seem to have been at Utterbach's, and then at the home of a family by the name of Grigsby.

Monday, September 30, 1861. Today Jackson rode down to the station and was very much surprised by the arrival of President Jefferson Davis in a single car. "He looked quite thin." The troops cheered him. Then the President got into an ambulance for the ride to Fairfax Court House. All along the way troops welcomed him with cheers. Soon a cavalry escort joined him. "It was quite an imposing pageant..."[6] for Jackson to watch.

Davis then reviewed the troops, and "took up his quarters with General Beauregard..." About 10:30 Jackson went to see him. The two talked about Union feeling in the western part of the state. Jackson stated his interest in the area, but Davis made no mention of the fact that he was thinking of sending Jackson there. The President spoke very highly of General Lee.

October 7, 1861. Near Fairfax. Jackson promoted to major-general.

Monday, October 21, 1861. The General wrote home today stating that he had been staying for several days with Mr. Grigsby. Jackson had one nice room, and the promise of the use of others. Tom was impressed with the library and the lovely portraits. Two sons of his host had come down with typhoid fever, but were over the critical stage. Mr. Grigsby had not yet consented to Jackson's staff moving into the house. This evening, Drs. White and McFarland arrived from Synod at Petersburg.

October 22, 1861. Jackson writes to Anna again, describing his quarters. He went into great detail. It was a brick house with four chimneys. The General's office was off a hallway to the right, with a hickory fire. Tom described the furnishings in almost as much depth as he would write a battlefield report. From the windows to the west, one could look upon the battlefield of Manassas.

Turning to military matters, Tom wanted a qualified staff person. He had written to Colonel Preston in Lexington.

Dr. White spent the day with him, and would stay another four. The pastor was gratified to find his friend having morning and evening devotions the same as he would at home. White led devotions for his parishioner until the last evening. Then he asked Jackson to have evening prayers. Dr. White said he would never forget the prayer as long as he lived.[7]

Jackson offered a real prayer of intercession, thanking God for sending White to visit the army, and for White's ministry in Lexington. He prayed for the Pastor's family and all the official members of the church. Jackson prayed that the Lord would give Dr. White many souls both at home and in his army travels. Finally, he pleaded with fervor that God would baptize the whole army with His Holy Spirit. White and Jackson talked till midnight.

Romney was the gateway to the Valley from the West. Control by the Yankees gave them an opportunity to repair the Baltimore and Ohio Railroad. It also meant harrassment of citizens known to be loyal to the South. On the other hand, but even more with Romney as a base, there was always a dagger pointed at the heart of the Valley, and the possibility of marching from Romney to a place like Staunton and launching a flank attack or a pincers movement on Richmond.

Confederate control meant protecting against this threat, and as long as the "Confederacy controlled the Valley," it could maintain a war in Virginia," and serve as a springboard for an invasion of the North. This happened when Lee marched to Gettysburg in 1863, and Early's march to the gates of

Washington in 1864. It was not until the autumn of '64 that Phil Sheridan completely destroyed the bread basket of the Confederacy. By then the South was running low on men, horses, and supplies. For a time Jubal Early put up a gallant fight, but at last he was overwhelmed.

But in the autumn of 1861, the star of the South was rising, and there was no talk of defeat. However, the folks in the western part of the state wanted protection. They clamored for a protector, leader, and someone who would deliver them from Yankee aggression. That man was Jackson.

On October 22, a Department of War comprising all of Virginia north of the Rappahannock River was created. Joseph E. Johnston was named overall commander. The Shenandoah was created as a separate district within Johnston's jurisdiction. It was a big area to oversee, stretching from the Alleghanies to the Blue Ridge, and running north and south from the Potomac River to Staunton. The area included 5,000 square miles. The responsibility for its protection was given to Jackson, largely because of his fame at Manassas, and because of the exploits of his Valley men.

Wednesday, October 23, 1861. Near Fairfax Court House.

Thursday, October 24, 1861. Near Fairfax.

Friday, October 25, 1861. Near Fairfax.

Saturday, October 26, 1861. Near Fairfax.

Sunday, October 27, 1861. Near Fairfax.

Monday, October 28, 1861. Near Fairfax.

Tuesday, October 29, 1861. Near Fairfax.

Wednesday, October 30, 1861. Near Fairfax. A grand review of all Virginia troops for Governor Letcher. The marching columns stretched over a mile. The bands played and the banners flew in the autumn air. Jackson, Lee, Longstreet, and many other officers were present.

Thursday, October 31, 1861. Near Fairfax.

Friday, November 1, 1861. Near Fairfax.

Saturday, November 2, 1861. Near Fairfax.

Sunday, November 3, 1861. Jackson's last full day at Fairfax Court House. Last minute attention given to details, getting ready to leave for Winchester.

Monday, November 4, 1861. Today, Thomas Jonathan Jackson bade a temporary farewell to "the Stonewall Brigade." In the morning, the regimental colonels came to say farewell. Their visit was followed by that of representatives of each company. The men in the ranks begged to see their beloved commander once again. At 1:00 p.m. Jackson rode behind the tents of the Second Virginia. Tears ran down the cheeks of the men. Jackson tells Hunter McGuire, "The name Stonewall belongs not to me, but to the brigade." Jackson then made a brief, but moving speech. Then not trusting his emotions, he responded to their cheers by waving his cap and riding off.[8]

Next it was on to Winchester, and the next phase of "Stonewall's" military career.

IV
WINCHESTER

As the train rolled across Virginia, traveling west to Strasburg, Jackson was headed for Winchester to spend the next three-and-one-half months of is life. He would lose the city in March, and then retake it in a brilliant victory in May.

In time, "no city in the whole Confederacy loved Jackson more whole heartedly, nor felt more deeply that he was its own particular savior..." After a while, Winchester became a second home to Tom Jackson.[1]

Winchester, the first city west of the Blue Ridge Mountains is a lovely place. Col. James Wood came in 1744. Soon Scotch-Irish folks followed, and the streets are named Cork, Amherst, Braddock, and Picadilly.

From this little village at the north end of the Shenandoah Valley, Goerge Washington surveyed the vast land holdings of Thomas Lord Fairfax. And after Braddock's defeat, Washington was named commander of Virginia's western frontier.

During the Civil War, Winchester was occupied by first one army, and then another. Jackson won a major victory in the area south of the present day Handley High School. General Ewell retook the city from the Yankees and General Milroy on the way to Gettysburg in June of 1863. And Phil Sheridan drove Early and his army from the city for good in September of 1864. A large Union, and a larger Confederate Cemetery are at the east end of town. But in the fall of 1861, Winchester was to be Jackson's city.

Tom Jackson rode away from the First Brigade accompanied by J.T.L. Preston and Sandie Pendleton. Apparently Jackson took the train from Manassas Junction to Strasburg, and then rode horseback to Winchester.

Tuesday, November 5, 1861. Reached Winchester early this morning, his base of operations for over four months.

Wednesday, November 6, 1861. Winchester.

Thursday, November 7, 1861. Winchester. And joy swept through the camp of the First Brigade as it was also ordered to Winchester.

Friday, November 8, 1861. Winchester. The Stonewall Brigade left their camps in the rain at Fairfax Court House, and marched to the trains at Manassas to head for Winchester.

Saturday, November 9, 1861. Winchester. Trains enroute from Manassas to Strasburg with the First Brigade. Heavy rain.

Sunday, November 10, 1861. Winchester. Last train bearing the Stonewall Brigade left Manassas at 8:30 a.m. Reached Strasburg at sundown.

Monday, November 11, 1861. Winchester. First Brigade marches from Strasburg to Winchester. A bright sun helps to dry their wet uniforms. Bivouac made near Kernstown.

Tuesday, November 12, 1861. Winchester. First Brigade in camp at Kernstown. Unhappy about being in a wet field.

Wednesday, November 13, 1861. Winchester. First Brigade marches to Winchester and northward to camp site several miles out on the Stephenson Road. Cold wind and bad weather.

Thursday, November 14, 1861. Winchester.

Friday, November 15, 1861. Winchester.

Saturday, November 16, 1861. Tom took up the pen to write to Anna. She apparently voiced the opinion that she wished he still had headquarters at Grigsbys. But Jackson assured her the place in Winchester was even better. "This house belongs to Lieutenant-Colonel Moore, of the Fourth Virginia Volunteers, and has a large yard around it. The situation is beautiful. (Visitors today would agree with that comment). The building is of cottage style and contains six rooms. I have two rooms, one above the other. My lower room, or office, has a matting on the floor, a large fine table, six chairs and a piano."[2]

The only thing missing was Mrs. Jackson. Today one can step back into the days of 1862 on Braddock Street in Winchester. That autumn, the home of Rev. and Mrs. James Graham[3] was just two doors away. And south of the Manse was the home of Dr. Hunter Holmes McGuire, Jackson's surgeon and friend.

Sunday, November 17, 1861. Winchester. Possibly heard Rev. James Graham preach for the first time.

Monday, November 18, 1861. Winchester. Provisional Congress of Confederacy meets in Richmond.

Tuesday, November 19, 1861. Winchester. Jefferson Davis addresses the Congress.

Wednesday, November 20, 1861. Winchester.

Thursday, November 21, 1861. Winchester.

Friday, November 22, 1861. Winchester.

Saturday, November 23, 1861. Winchester.

Sunday, November 24, 1861. Winchester.

Monday, November 25, 1861. Winchester.

Tuesday, November 26, 1861. Winchester.

Wednesday, November 27, 1861. Winchester.

Thursday, November 28, 1861. Winchester.

Friday, November 29, 1861. Winchester.

Saturday, November 30, 1861. Winchester.

—————December 1861—————

The last month in the year found Jackson in Winchester. He wrote to obtain a new commander for the Stonewall Brigade, made an attempt to destroy Dam No. 5, received his wife, and put the finishing touches on his plans to attack Romney.

Sunday, December 1, 1861. Winchester.

Monday, December 2, 1861. Winchester. Jackson writes to Richmond seeking a good commander for the Stonewall Brigade.

Tuesday, December 3, 1861. Winchester.

Wednesday, December 4, 1861. Winchester. Richard B. Garnett was assigned to command the Stonewall Brigade. He had been a good field commander, seeing action with Sixth U.S. Cavalry.

Thursday, December 5, 1861. Winchester.

Friday, December 6, 1861. Winchester.

Saturday, December 7, 1861. Winchester. Today, Richard B. Garnett,[4] a West Point graduate and veteran of twenty years on frontier posts took command of the Stonewall Brigade. He made a good impression on the men.

Sunday, December 8, 1861. Winchester.

Monday, December 9, 1861. Winchester.

Tuesday, December 10, 1861. Winchester.

Wednesday, December 11, 1861. Winchester.

Thursday, December 12, 1861. Winchester.

Friday, December 13, 1861. Winchester.

Saturday, December 14, 1861. Winchester.

Sunday, December 15, 1861. Winchester. Making final plans for the expedition against the C and O Canal.[5]

——December 16-23, 1861. Canal expedition.——

Running from Washington to Cumberland, a distance of 185 miles is the Chesapeake and Ohio Canal, a magnificent engineering feat, opened on July 4, 1828, to take fresh produce to western Maryland, and return with coal from the hills of Maryland.

Earlier Jackson had disrupted traffic on the B and O Railroad. Now the canal was to feel his wrath. The canal took twenty-two years to build, cost $22 million, and the efforts of 6,000 workers along the banks on the Potomac on the Maryland side of the river.

Different dams supplied water to the canal in times of low flow, and lakes formed behind the dam, made it possible to tow boats along the river bank, thus saving miles of digging and cost. Several miles west of Williamsport, Maryland is Dam No. 5. Jackson decided this was the nearest and most feasible place to wreck havoc.

Monday, December 16, 1861. The Stonewall Brigade left camp, and marched fifteen miles to Martinsburg. There they rested for a while, before proceeding another thirteen miles to the bluffs overlooking the Potomac River and Dam No. 5. All baggage, tents and wagons had been left at Big Spring.

Tuesday, December 17, 1861. Near Dam No. 5. Jackson kept his men hidden throughout the day waiting for the cover of darkness. When night fell, thirty members of the New Market Irishmen made their way to the middle of the dam and started to hack away at the Dam. It was bitterly cold.

Wednesday, December 18, 1861. At Dam No. 5. The Confederates seeking to destroy the Dam were discovered at daybreak. Jackson ordered the Rockbridge Artillery and Chew's Battery to open fire on the Yankees sniping at the men in the river. The Yankees replied with artillery of their own. Jackson suspended operations until dark. However, when night fell, Union artillery lobbed shells into the old mill on the Virginia side of the river where Jackson's men were waiting to resume their work of destruction.

Thursday, December 19, 1861. At Dam No. 5, waiting for the proper moment to resume the work of destruction again. When night fell, Jackson moved some men up the river. The Yankees thought he was leaving, and was heading for Dam No. 4. They left too. Immediately Jackson had others get to work on Dam No. 5. The men worked without any attack from the enemy. The only problem, the ice cold water.[6]

Friday, December 20, 1861. At Dam No. 5.

Saturday, December 21, 1861. Jackson and his men retrace their steps to Winchester.

Sunday, December 22, 1861. On the way back to Winchester from Dam No. 5.

Monday, December 23, 1861. The last miles from the Potomac to Winchester are completed.

Tuesday, December 24, 1861. Winchester.

Wednesday, December 25, 1861. Jackson spends Christmas with his wife, the last time they would be together for the birthday of the Christ child.

Thursday, December 26, 1861. In Winchester.

Friday, December 27, 1861. In Winchester.

Saturday, December 28, 1861. Winchester.

Sunday, December 29, 1861. Winchester.

Monday, December 30, 1861. Winchester.

Tuesday, December 31, 1861. Winchester, on the eve of the
greatest year in his life.

———— The Year in Summary ————

The end of April, all of May, and the first half of June at Harpers
Ferry. The last half of June and early July, on patrol from Bunker
Hill north to the Potomac, with the first action occurring at Falling
Waters.

Then it was on to Winchester, across the mountains and fame at
Manassas. The rest of July, August, September and October were
spent at Fairfax Court House and in the Centreville area.

November brought assignment to Winchester and command of
the Valley District. Jackson left for his new duties on November 4,
and established headquarters in Winchester on November 6.

Wednesday, January 1, 1862. A new day and a new year brought a
new campaign. This was the expedition to Romney. It began in
sunshine and ended in snow and ice. Some would compare it
with Napolean's Moscow experience.

Loring's men and the Stonewall Brigade were ordered to
march at an early hour on nearly parallel roads. But there was
a late start. The morning was nice for the first of January. But
then the wind got up and the temperature dropped, and still
later snow fell. As a result, a scant eight miles were covered,
and by night fall the command was at Pughtown. The troops
suffered in the dark from the icy winds. Before he left, Jackson
asked Rev. Graham if Anna could lodge at the Manse.

Thursday, January 2, 1862. Jackson continued deeper into the
mountains. Rough roads caused many wagons to break down.
Another eight miles were covered, and the troops reached
Unger's Store.

Friday, January 3, 1862. Heading north, Jackson reached a point across from Bath, modern day Berkeley Springs. He wanted to surprise and capture Union troops there and at Hancock, Maryland, clearing them of enemy forces, protecting his flank, and disrupting the B and O. Tom had a good plan, but the men moved slowly, and they also ran into a Yankee outpost. By dark the command was at the outskirts of Bath, but they had to halt for the night. And more snow fell.[7]

Saturday, January 4, 1862. Bath fell to Jackson, and the Yankees were chased to the Potomac. Jackson called for the surrender of Hancock, but was refused. The Union commander was given two hours to remove the women and children. A few shells were lobbed into the town. Jackson was experiencing trouble with Loring's Brigade, they were not used to a man like him, and they certainly were not equal to the Stonewall Brigade.

Sunday, January 5, 1862. Arkansas troops burned the big railroad bridge over the Great Cacapon River. A canal dam was breached, and a lot of damage done to the B and O tracks. Union communications were disrupted. More snow fell, and old timers called it one of the worst winters ever. The pickets almost froze.

Monday, January 6, 1862. Union reinforcements at Hancock forced Jackson to abandon thoughts of crossing the Potomac, and his troops opposite the town were withdrawn.

Tuesday, January 7, 1862. The column turned south. There was a surprise skirmish at Hanging Rock Pass which caused Jackson great alarm. Weather turned bad once again. There was a terrible ice storm, and the men could barely stand. The temperature dropped below zero. Camp was made at Unger's Store. The men had to be rested, and the horses refitted. Jackson helped push wagons on the slippery roads.

Wednesday, January 8, 1862. The command remained halted at Unger's Store. Even Major Paxton of the 27th Virginia thought that Jackson would see the futility of the campaign and put the men in winter quarters. Loring had 800 men ill. Dr. McGuire had 1,300 sick in Winchester. Temporarily things ground to a halt. Jackson realized his men had not bathed in a long time. Water was heated and men bathed to get rid of lice.

Thursday, January 9, 1862. At Unger's Store.

Friday, January 10, 1862. At Unger's Store.

Saturday, January 11, 1862. At Unger's Store.

Sunday, January 12, 1862. At Unger's Store.

Monday, January 13, 1862. The march was resumed for Romney. The sun was shining and things looked good. Once again a storm developed.

Tuesday, January 14, 1862. Rain and sleet buffeted the men on the way to Romney.

Wednesday, January 15, 1862. Jackson's command reached Romney. All along the way they saw desolation by the Yankees. They also heard stories of the harassment of Southern sympathizers.

Thursday, January 16, 1862. In Romney. Loring's men arrived today. Jackson wanted to strike Cumberland and the B and O stores in that city. However, he could not obtain reinforcements.

Friday, January 17, 1862. In Romney. The General gave orders to strike the New Creek railroad bridge and disrupt the B and O. He had a problem though, the Stonewall Brigade had suffered greatly on the march and was under strength. Thus the strike had to be canceled. Company C of the 23rd Virginia had but fifteen men able to walk.

Saturday, January 18, 1862. In Romney. Jackson, realizing he had achieved about all he could hope for with the men and materials at his command, placed his units in winter quarters at Bath and Moorefield. Loring's command held Romney. They called it a pig pen.

Sunday, January 19, 1862. Romney.

Monday, January 20, 1862. Romney.

Tuesday, January 21, 1862. Today, Garnett and the Stonewall Brigade left Romney for Winchester. This angered Loring's men. They called Garnett's troops, "Jackson's pet lambs." Jackson also left Romney. This may have been the night Hunter McGuire gave Jackson something to drink, warming him so that he opened his coat. The staff had to admonish him to close it for fear of catching cold.

Jackson's 38th birthday.

Thursday, January 23, 1862. On the road to Winchester, following what is roughly U.S. 50 today. Once again the command saw the burned out homes along the way. They also saw evidence of looting, and the slaughter of livestock. Jackson arrived in Winchester late in the evening, went to headquarters to clean up, and then went hurrying to Rev. Graham's to see his beloved wife. Back home with her he said, "This is the essence of comfort.[8]

Friday, January 24, 1862. In Winchester. Jackson made his lodging at Graham's too.

Saturday, January 25, 1862. In Winchester. Garnett's troops arrive. Town filled with sick and suffering soldiers.

Sunday, January 26, 1862. In Winchester.

Monday, January 27, 1862. In Winchester.

Tuesday, January 28, 1862. In Winchester.

Wednesday, January 29, 1862. In Winchester.

Thursday, January 30, 1862. In Winchester. Loring and Jackson had been at odds during the expedition. And on January 22 Loring and his officers signed a petition and sent it to Secretary of War Benjamin. They knew it was useless to go through channels. Besides, Jackson to them was cold and stern.[9]

In a reply to the request from Romney, Benjamin sent a directive to Jackson, dated this 30th day of January. It was curt. "Our news indicates that a movement is being made to cut off General Loring's command. Order him back to Winchester immediately."

Friday, January 31, 1862. In Winchester. The Romney expedition was tough. And it produced much grumbling, or groaning and growling as soldiers say. Abram Miller wrote that 2,000 were on the sick list. He stated that they were out sixteen days and only rested three. He lost his voice and stood more cold than he ever thought he could stand. He suffered some frost bite, and begged his relatives to send him some wool shirts.

Years later William Poague, a member of the Rockbridge Artillery states, "In all the war I never had a similar experience — never endured such physical and mental suffering...The expedition seemed to everybody to be a dismal failure. Our confidence in our leader was sorely tried. Loring's part of the army was in a state of semi-mutiny and Jackson was hissed and hooted at as he passed by them." Friends teased Poague about "the crazy general from Richmond."[10]

William Casler said, "We were out nearly one month, and had miserable weather all the time...We lost more men from sickness than if we had been engaged in a big battle. We accomplished nothing, for the enemy retreated across the Potomac, only to come back again as soon as we left. Winchester was full of soldiers sick with pneumonia, and they died by the hundreds."[11] Some rest at the Stonewall Cemetery in Winchester, Casler fell sick on February 1, and did not get out until Winchester was evacuated.

With this feeling in the army and trouble in Richmond, Jackson sent a message to Secretary of War Benjamin.

Sir: Your order requiring me to direct General Loring to return with his command to Winchester immediately has been received and promptly complied with.

With such interference in my command I cannot expect to be of much service in the field, and accordingly, respectfully request to be ordered to report for duty to the Superintendent of the Virginia Military Institute at Lexington...Should this application not be granted, I respectfully request that the President will accept my resignation from the Army...[12]

So this was the day the Confederacy and history almost lost Thomas Jonathan Jackson. His tone sounded somewhat like that of Patton and MacArthur in our day.

Tom also sent another message to his friend Governor Letcher, talking about political interference and the fact that Benjamin made the decision about Loring without consulting him. He asked the governor to do him a special favor and order him back to VMI.

All of this happened as Jackson opened the mail at the start of his day at headquarters. He stayed and wrote the two letters and then went back to Grahams for breakfast with Anna. He mentioned that they might soon be back in Lexington, but did not say why.

Headquarters in Winchester, November 1861-March 10, 1862.
(Courtesy Ben Ritter)

February 1862

Later in the year, the winter of 1862-1863, Jackson was to spend approximately ninety days at Moss Neck near Fredericksburg. In terms of a long stay at one place, Winchester is tops on the list. However, February of 1862, was the only complete month Jackson spent in the city he grew to love. He was in Winchestesr for twenty-five days in November of 1862, another twenty-five in December of that year, eight in January of '62, all of February and the first ten days in March. This makes a total of ninety-six days. December and January brought the foray against Dam No. 5 in Maryland and the Romney Expedition.

Letters continued to go back and forth from Jackson to Richmond about his command performance and return to VMI. As always, he was willing to accept whatever developed. And this turned out to be a lovely time with his wife who was staying just down the street from headquarters. February 1862 was like an oasis in the desert, or the calm before the storm. Mrs. Jackson describes those days:

> The Winchester ladies were among the most famous of Virginia housekeepers and lived in a great deal of old-fashioned elegance and profusion. The old border town had not then changed hands with the conflicting armies, as it was destined to do many times during the war. Under the rose-colored light in which I viewed everything that winter, it seemed to me that no people could have been more cultivated, attractive and noble-hearted. The memories of that sojourn in our 'war home' are among the most precious and sacred of my whole life. It was there that I was permitted to be the longest time with my husband after he entered the army.[13]

And during February, Mrs. Jackson became pregnant.

Saturday, February 1, 1862. In Winchester. Jackson's letter to Gov. Letcher was in the mail today. It said essentially the same as the one to Secretary Benjamin. Although Tom mailed it Friday, he was thinking about the contents of both letters on this first day of February.

Jackson was furious that Romney was ordered evacuated without his consultation. He felt

> (we are) abandoning to the enemy what has cost much preparation, expense and exposure to secure, and is in direct conflict with my military plans, and implies a want of confidence in my ability to judge when General Loring's troops should fall back, and is an attempt to control military operations in detail from the Secretary's desk at a distance...[14]

This is an old problem. The military still has problems with control from high government sources.

Joseph E. Johnston wrote a letter to Jackson asking that he reconsider. He said ordinarily this was the right course to follow. But they were now engaged in war and in great danger, and Jackson was needed. Johnston also felt insulted because he did not receive a copy of the original order which he should have been sent.

Governor Letcher was dismayed when he received Jackson's letter. He rushed over to Secretary Benjamin's office. Now it was the cabinet official's time to squirm. The governor said Jackson was a valuable man and the Confederacy could not afford to let him go. Letcher then asked Benjamin to do nothing until he could communicate with Jackson. The secretary agreed.

Colonel A.R. Boteler[15] was a congressman and close friend of the Jacksons. Perhaps the General would listen to Boteler. Boteler could not leave right away, so he sent a letter.

Jackson held firm. "I hold to the opinion that a man should be in a position where he can be most useful. And I do not see how I can be of any service in the field, so long as that principle which has been applied to me — of undoing at the War Department what is done in the field — is adhered to."

In Winchester. Colonel Boteler arrives, goes to Jackson's headquarters and talks far into the night. Virginia needs all her sons. No one has the right to quit and go home. He appealed to Jackson in the name of the great State of Virginia, not to desert her in the hour of need.

Sunday, February 2, 1862. Winchester.

Monday, February 3, 1862. Winchester.

Tuesday, February 4, 1862. Winchester.

Wednesday, February 5, 1862. Winchester. Joseph E. Johnston wrote to President Davis in behalf of Jackson, and also requesting that he be relieved from command of the Valley District if there was going to be interference from Richmond.

Thursday, February 6, 1862. Winchester. Jackson writes once again to Governor Letcher. He is beginning to mellow and cool down. He also sees the esteem in which he is held, and states that if leaving the service would produce a harmful effect upon the service, he will stay. The crisis was over. We dwell on this because during these days the South almost lost Jackson.

Friday, February 7, 1862. Winchester. Jackson had not changed his mind about Loring. His actions in refusing to go through channels was a serious breech of military procedure. Jackson therefore requested a military court martial for General Loring. General Johnston felt it should be held in the Valley District to maintain discipline.

Jackson charged Loring with failure to care for his men in camp, and with failure to attack and press the enemy when ordered to do so. Jackson was also upset over the long and frequent halts, Loring ordered on the march. Loring was questioned, and sent elsewhere.

Saturday, February 8, 1862. Winchester.

Sunday, February 9, 1862. Winchester.

Tuesday, February 11, 1862. Winchester. Jackson relaxed a little and permitted the men to go to town. Some rode in sleighs. Naturally, they tried to impress the ladies. And Rev. Pendleton constructed a chapel.

Wednesday, February 12, 1862. Winchester.

Thursday, February 13, 1862. Winchestser.

Friday, February 14, 1862. Winchester.

Saturday, February 15, 1862. Winchester.

Sunday, February 16, 1862. Winchester.

Monday, February 17, 1862. Winchester.

Tuesday, February 18, 1862. Winchester.

Wednesday, February 19, 1862. In Winchester.

Thursday, February 20, 1862. In Winchester.

Friday, February 21, 1862. In Winchester.

Saturday, February 22, 1862. In Winchester.

Sunday, February 23, 1862. In Winchester. Today Union forces began moving, following Lincoln's directive of January 27, "directing all federal land and naval forces to move against insurgent forces."

Monday, February 24, 1862. In Winchester.

Tuesday, February 25, 1862. In Winchester. Today, James Keith Boswell reported for duty with Jackson. He was introduced by Lt. Junkin. Jackson arose and shook hands and asked Boswell to be seated. The General wanted to know when the young man had left Richmond. Then he said there was a task to be done. The enemy had crossed at Harpers Ferry and a high wind was preventing reinforcements from crossing. Boswell was to see if the Union force could be captured. He also wanted to know if Boswell had a horse and where the horse was. Then Jackson made a remark heard often by those around him; when Boswell asked when he should leave, Jackson replied, "As soon as possible."[16]
He was given letters of introduction to Captain Baylor and Colonel Botts in Charles Town. And then Boswell, who would later be gunned down with his commander, left on his first reconnaissance for General Jackson. Before the day was over he saw Yankee soldiers for the first time, and tomorrow he would come under fire.

Wednesday, February 26, 1862. Winchester. Today, General N.P. Banks,[17] in compliance with Lincoln's orders crossed the pontoon bridge at Harpers Ferry ready to move against Jackson, Winchester and the Valley. McClellan came by train to Sandy Hook to watch the crossing.

Thursday, February 27, 1862. Winchester.

Friday, February 28, 1862. Winchester. A day of fasting and prayer in the Confederacy.

Saturday, March 1, 1862. Winchester.

Sunday, March 2, 1862. Winchester.

Monday, March 3, 1862. Winchester.

Tuesday, March 4, 1862. Winchester.

Wednesday, March 5, 1862. Winchester.

Thursday, March 6, 1862. Winchester.

Friday, March 7, 1862. In Winchester. Nathaniel P. Banks, former politician from Massachusetts was heading southward toward Winchester. The time for the spring offensive had come. Ashby's cavalry had a lively skirmish with the Yanks. Jackson spread a thin line of infantry about two miles north of his headquarters. Major John Harman was busy crating the army supplies to head south. Harman also received an order from Jackson telling him to "send his wagon to headquarters; this looks like we are about to be off....What is to become of us, God only knows."

Saturday, March 8, 1862. In Winchester, but the situation deteriorating. Major Harman said, "The crisis is upon us. Everything is packed and ready for a move. Jackson will certainly make a stand if he can do it without the risk being too great."

Sunday, March 9, 1862. In Winchester. Couriers coming and going from Jackson's headquarters. No one knew how long they would be able to stay. It all depended on the Yankee advance and what they did. Jackson wanted to stay, but he was very weak in numbers. Shields had come from Paw Paw to Bath and thence to Martinsburg to reinforce Banks. The Union force was an estimated 40,000. Jackson had less than 4,000.

With the coming of March, it was time to launch the spring offensive. One Union objective was Richmond. The other thrust was to control or protect "the back door" to Washington. Therefore, General Nathaniel P. Banks was placed in command of about 38,000 men in the Harpers Ferry area.

Banks was ordered to drive Jackson from the Shenandoah Valley, and then head eastward in a great pincers movement and cooperate with McClellan and his attack on Richmond.

Jackson had less than 5,000 effective men as March began. When he left Winchester on the 11th, Banks was so sure of his success that he sent some of his army to Washington.

Banks counted his chickens before they hatched. He stopped pursuing Jackson about forty miles south of Winchester. Immediately Jackson turned and headed after Banks. His purpose was to pose as much alarm, and tie up as many Union troops as possible. The movement resulted in the battle of Kernstown on March 23. Although Jackson lost his only engagement of the war, he achieved a tactical victory, sending fear to Washington, and causing the Federal government to send a large number of troops after him. More about that in April.

V
THE VALLEY CAMPAIGN

Monday, March 10, 1862. Word arrived from scouts that the Yankees were within five miles of Winchester. Sometimes you have to retreat in order to advance. This is what Jackson did, or was preparing to do.

Tuesday, March 11, 1862. Jackson's command prepared for action and was on the alert. However, the Union General Banks awaited the arrival of reinforcements. Late afternoon Jackson called at the home of the Graham's dressed in his boots, spurs, military cloak and dress sword. Jackson joined them for the evening meal and remained for family prayers, dressed for combat. Then he asked for a lunch to be placed in his haversack.

His next stop was a council of war at headquarters, north of Grahams. He had hoped to launch a surprise night attack. He was upset to find that the officers had already placed some columns in line of march to the rear. His lieutenants felt the men were too tired and had marched too much during the day. Jackson paced the floor trying to seek a way to prevent the fall of Winchester. The candles made an eerie light on his face. However, it looked as though all he could do was to fall back. Jackson bade a sad farewell to his friends, and then rode out of town. South of the town, he and Hunter McGuire looked northward to the city from a hill and the General said, "That's the last council of war I'll ever hold."

Wednesday, March 12, 1862. On the march to Strasburg.[1]

Thursday, March 13, 1862. Jackson's command continued its strategic withdrawal toward Mt. Jackson.[2]

Friday, March 14, 1862. On the road to Mount Jackson.

Saturday, March 15, 1862. Woodstock.

Sunday, March 16, 1862. Woodstock.

Monday, March 17, 1862. By now most of the command was at Mount Jackson. The next several days were to be good for them. They regrouped, got some rest and had good rations and campsites, thanks to the pre-planning of Major Hawks. Jackson wrote to his wife from Woodstock.

Tuesday, March 18, 1862. In the Mount Jackson area.

Wednesday, March 19, 1862. In the Mount Jackson area.

Thursday, March 20, 1862. Near Mount Jackson.

Friday, March 21, 1862. Today Jackson received a dispatch from Ashby saying that Shields had left Strasburg.

Saturday, March 22, 1862. Once again the men of Jackson were on the march. They left Mount Jackson and headed for Strasburg, twenty-six miles away. All day long the columns pressed northward. Jackson was constantly saying, "Press on. Press on." Depending on where they were in column of march, the men covered twenty-one to twenty-six miles. Headquarters were made in Strasburg.

Sunday, March 23, 1862. Battle of Kernstown. This was a day of decision for Jackson. It was the Sabbath, and the general was opposed to fighting on the Lord's Day, but it looked like a necessity. Marching orders were issued, and at the crack of dawn, weary men of the "Stonewall Brigade" were back on the road. About 2:00 p.m. Garnett's men approached the village of Kernstown, "a hamlet of a dozen houses, sealed in the midst of meadows, three miles from Winchester."[3]

Once again Jackson gave some thought to fighting on Sunday, but he felt he had no alternative. Writing to Anna later, he said, "I felt it my duty to do it,...though very distasteful to my feelings; and I hope and pray to our heavenly Father that I may never again be circumstanced as on that day....Necessity and mercy called for the battle...."[4]

Bivouac orders were canceled and the battle begun. 2,700 Confederates attacked 11,000 Yankees. Jackson felt that with another 2,000 men he would have won. And his troops were tired.

Jackson lost the battle. Yet it was a tactical success. His efforts caused Lincoln to send three armies after him, and his small command was to tie up over 60,000 Union troops for several months and prevent McClellan from being reinforced. Jackson, who had lost one-fourth of his command, gave orders for the wounded to be gathered at Middletown, south of the field of action. The ambulance people worked through the night. Dr. McGuire asked, "Can you stay to protect us?"

Jackson replied, "Make yourself easy. The army stays here till the last wounded man is recovered."[5]

One of the sad results of this battle was the feud that developed between Jackson and Garnett over the latter's withdrawal from combat. The men were out of ammunition, but Jackson felt they should have used the bayonet. The exhausted command falls back to Newton, now Stephens City.

Monday, March 24, 1862. The General orders his command back to Mount Jackson.

Tuesday, March 25, 1862. Jackson's army was on the road "Column South."

Wednesday, March 26, 1862. Headquarters was located at the Stover's along the Valley Pike, and just south of Narrow Passage. This was a big day in the life of General Jackson. The commander sent for Jed Hotchkiss and discussed his topographical work on northwestern Virginia the previous year. Jackson sad to him, "I want you to make me a map of the Valley, from Harper's Ferry to Lexington, showing all the points of offense and defense in those places. Mr. Pendleton will give orders for whatever outfit you need."[6] This was the beginning of Jed's career as Jackson's map maker.

Thursday, March 27, 1862. Headquarters, Narrow Passage. Today General Jackson received a letter from Mrs. Lee in Winchester stating that the Mayor and the ladies of the town had buried the Confederates who had been killed at the Battle of Kernstown.

Friday, March 28, 1862. Near Mount Jackson. Tom wrote to his wife from the home of a Mr. Allen where he was quite comfortable. Jackson was much impressed with the country, particularly the Meems farm. He expressed the desire that his wife could tour the lovely area with him.

Saturday, March 29, 1862. Near Mount Jackson.

Sunday, March 30, 1862. Near Mount Jackson.

Monday, March 31, 1862. Near Mount Jackson.

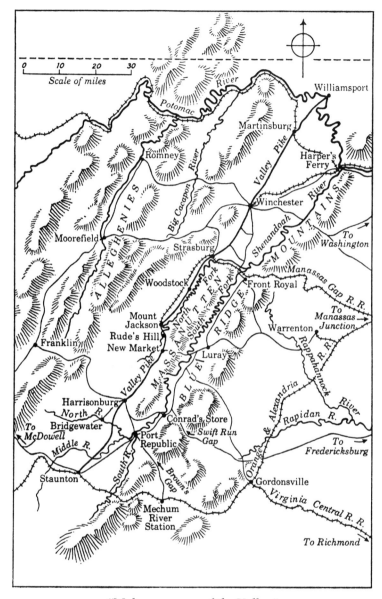

"Make me a map of the Valley"
Words spoken to Jed Hotchkiss at Narrow Passage, March 26, 1862.

John W. Schildt   45

——————— April 1862 ———————

Kernstown made Lincoln and his government, "stop, look and listen." They were not exactly sure who this man Jackson was, but they were afraid of him.

During April, Banks regrouped in Winchester and then started after Jackson once again. In so doing, he got farther and farther from his base of supplies. It took several weeks for Banks to reach Harrisonburg, seventy miles south of Winchester. All along the way there was constant skirmishing with Ashby, Jackson's cavalry leader.

At the same time, John C. Fremont, "The Pathfinder," and the Republican presidential candidate in 1856, led a column against Jackson from the mountains of West Virginia. Jackson now had 17,000 men. But if Fremont and Banks united, they would have 35,000 men. Jackson was determined to "divide and conquer," and prevent them from joining forces.

In late April, Jackson "assumed the offensive and began that succession of movements which ended in the complete derangement of the Union plans in Virginia — on the Peninsula as well as the Shenandoah."

Jackson had some advantages. He was leading Virginians and these men were fighting for their homeland. He also knew the Valley and was aided by the maps of Jed Hotchkiss and other officers who knew all the back roads and secluded avenues of approach. Someone said, "he knows even the cowpaths through the woods and the goat tracks along the hills." Friendly civilians were also ready to pass on everything they saw and heard.

This month was spent in regrouping at Mount Jackson, and then the latter half of the month began the series of marches which confounded the enemy and let to Jackson's successes in May.

Tuesday, April 1, 1862. Jackson and Jed Hotchkiss studied the map of the Stony Creek area. Jed reported on his personal scouting expedition of the previous day. Jackson decided against the Narrow Passage line[6] and sent Jed to tell Col. Ashby to hold at Stony Creek. Ashby had already been driven back through Edinburg. He burned the bridge, and with horse artillery on the hill was able to hold the line.

A little boy followed Ashby and had his horse "Dixie" shot and killed. The main army fell back through Narrow Passage and marched through Woodstock.

Headquarters was at Israel Allen's near Hawkinsville. Most of the staff slept on the ground.

Wednesday, April 2, 1862. Jackson spent half the day at the Stony Creek line of defense at Edinburg. A small detachment of infantry and Ashby's cavalry skirmished with the Yankees most of the day. Riding back to headquarters at Rev. Rude's, Jackson said, "We have been favored by Providence today. "Not only had his troops held, but the General had survived several nearby shell burst. Pastor Rude lived at "Locust Grove," at the foot of Rude's Hill.

Thursday, April 3, 1862. Jackson worked at Rude's. The staff was busy but took time to get acquainted with the family. Most of the staff slept in one large room, many of them rolled up in blankets on the floor.

Friday, April 4, 1862. Jackson spent most of his time in his room at Rude's, apparently writing his report of the Battle of Kernstown." He is very quiet, says but little and eats but little." Jed Hotchkiss notes that the General has a problem with deafness.

Saturday, April 5, 1862. At Rude's.

Sunday, April 6, 1862. At Rude's. A nice spring day. The grain and the grass were turning green. Flowers were starting to appear on the earth. It did not seem like war. Tom said, "It was a lovely Sabbath day. I did not have the privilege of going to church. Yet it felt like a holy Sabbath day, beautiful serene and lovely. All I wanted was the church bell and God's services in the sanctuary to make it complete."[7]

Monday, April 7, 1862. Headquarters still at Rude's.

Tuesday, April 8, 1862. At Rude's. Mr. Rude was a retired Lutheran pastor, a Dane by birth. He married the widow Steenbergen. The couple was extremely nice to Jackson and his staff.

Wednesday, April 9, 1862. At Rude's. More rain. Hard for morale and difficult for the troops.

Thursday, April 10, 1862. Still at Rude's. It rained for the third day. Everything was soggy. And although Jackson at times seems cold and stern, he was always concerned about weather conditions and their effect on the troops. Jackson must have been grateful for the comfort of the Rude home. Jed wrote home saying he felt the Staunton area was safe. "I have great confidence in our generals, and think the Valley will not be given up."

Friday, April 11, 1862. At Rude's. The spring rain continued. It must have been like equinox.

Saturday, April 12, 1862. At Rude's. The rains abated somewhat today, just showers.

Sunday, April 13, 1862. This was the Sabbath. And Jackson went to one of the brigade camps near Rude's and distributed religious tracts. William B. Taliaferro reported for duty. This did not make Jackson very happy. Taliaferro had not done well in the Romney expedition and sided with Loring. Yet Jackson was guarded in his remarks about the officers. It seems as though that he could rake a man over the coals, doing it face to face, but said little about the person behind his back. Jed Hotchkiss says, "I do not remember to have ever heard him say ought in derogation of anyone, at any time.[8]

Monday, April 14, 1862. Still at Rude's and more rain. The waters were high, the ground was soaked, and campsites were a sea of mud. Headquarters staff lamented the deaths of the two children of Major John A. Harman. Scarlet fever was very bad at the time.

Jed has an interesting description of Jackson. "I am very much pleased with General Jackson and his staff. He is at times very chatty, but usually has but little to say....He stays to himself most of the time; eats very sparingly; does not drink tea or coffee and eats scarcely any meat." The Rude's were having trouble pronouncing Jed's name. One of the girls called him "Mr. Lipkiss."

Tuesday, April 15, 1862. At Rude's. Weather finally showed signs of breaking.

Wednesday, April 16, 1862. Still at Rude's, although the time was about at an end.

Thursday, April 17, 1862. The last day at Rude's. Union forces advanced at 3:00 a.m., compelling the Confederates to retire from the Stony Creek line which they had held since April 1. As soon as word came from Ashby, the headquarter's wagons were sent to the rear. Jed Hotchkiss rode around to the flank of the mountain and watched the Union deployment, and then gave his report to Jackson. Ashby tried to burn the bridge over the North River, but it did not burn quickly enough and Union cavalry galloped across, inflicting a mortal wound on his lovely white horse. Jackson fell back to New Market and presented a line of battle there. The night was spent at Mr. Lincoln's, a distant relative of the President. Mrs. Lincoln wanted to know if General Jackson was any relation to "the other Jackson who used to stop here?" She was referring to "Old Hickory." Stonewall, being a Democrat and a strong admirer of the former President was pleased with the question. The folks in the New Market area were very disturbed by the Confederate retreat. Col. J.T.L. Preston rejoined Jackson. Jackson and the staff were sorry to leave Rude's. Although Jed was very anxious and did not know what was going to happen, he said, "Jackson is very cautious and I do not think he will be caught napping."

Friday, April 18, 1862. On the road. Jackson was up early, giving personal instructions to quartermasters and brigades. He and the staff "rode rapidly to Harrisonburg....The troops cheered the General lustily as we rode by them while on the march." Jackson and his staff dined at "Hill Top" the home of Rev. William Henry Ruffner. He stayed for awhile to observe from the hill. Then he rode to Keezletown and took quarters at Mr. Peale's. The advance of the army arrived in the area. The Peale home was six miles from Harrisonburg.

Saturday, April 19, 1862. On the march. Near Conrad's Store, modern day Elkton.

Sunday, April 20, 1862. Easter Sunday. "The army rested in camp." Ashby's cavalry was near Conrad's Store, with his pickets in near McGaheysville. The bulk of the infantry was near Elk Run Church. The weather was bad. There was rain, and the mud was terrible. Jed Hotchkiss felt, "The war is only just begun and Heaven only can tell what the future has in store for us....No matter how dark the heavens may now appear they must become brighter, and through the thick gloom I think we may see the glimmerings of a brighter dawn. God grant that it may come soon."

Monday, April 21, 1862. Conrad's Store - Elk Run area. More rain today.

Tuesday, April 22, 1862. Conrad's Store - Elk Run.

Wednesday, April 23, 1862. Conrad's Store - Elk Run.

Thursday, April 24, 1862. Conrad's Store - Elk Run. Rev. R.L. Dabney reported for duty as Assistant Adjutant General of the Valley District.[9] Tonight, Jackson and Turner Ashby had a long talk. There was snow today. Ewell's army was now within supporting distance. Most of Jackson's discussion with Ashby was over the division of his command into two regiments. Ashby did not like the idea.

Friday, April 25, 1862. Conrad's Store - Elk Run area.

Saturday, April 26, 1862. Conrad's Store - Elk Run area.

Sunday, April 27, 1862. Conrad's Store - Elk Run area.

Monday, April 28, 1862. Conrad's Store - Elk Run area.

Tuesday, April 29, 1862. Conrad's Store - Elk Run area.

Wednesday, April 30, 1862. Conrad's Store - Elk Run area. Port Republic at night.

Thursday, May 1, 1862. This was another miserable day. During the next eight weeks, Jackson and his army were pelted many times with heavy rain, and this was one of those days. The Virginia roads were terrible. Jackson and "all the staff spent the day with large details of soldiers making and repairing roads and helping the wagons and artillery along through the mud and quicksands." They made but five miles. Headquarters was established at Lewiston.

Friday, May 2, 1862. Jackson spent the day working on the roads and helping his wagon trains. "By desperate efforts we got the trains and troops, by way of opposite Port Royal, into the entrance to Brown's Gap." The cavalry arrived and camped near Port Republic. Jackson stopped at the home of John F. Lewis at Mt. Vernon Furnace, three miles from Port Republic. Hotchkiss and Boswell had supervised the Virginia troops in road building throughout the day. They took supper at Madison Hall, the home of Dr. George W. Kemper, Sr. The sunny day helped dry up some of the mud.

Saturday, May 3, 1862. Jackson had his troops on the road early in the morning. They crossed Brown's Gap, heading for the Virginia Central station at Mechum River. Once again "Old Jack" was concealing his intentions. Some thought he might be headed for Richmond. Others guessed they were on the way to

Staunton. After eating at the home of John F. Lewis, Jackson and his staff followed the troops and joined them at the foot of Brown's Gap. The men were washing the mud from themselves and their ragged uniforms in a cold stream on the eastern slope of the mountain. The General seemed to enjoy the ride. Jackson watched them for awhile, then headed for the railroad depot.

Sunday, May 4, 1862. On this Sabbath, the men under T.J. Jackson boarded trains and headed for Staunton. They had been under a severe strain. Major Harman had sent reckless letters leaking information and saying the town was doomed. This had brought a severe reprimand from Jackson. Ed Johnson had been west of town watching the Union advance. But this night Johnson and his men were in Staunton. It was a short night, for at 2:00 a.m. Johnson was called to advance to meet the Union threat. Heavy fighting occurred. The folks in Staunton were worried. Afternoon came. They didn't know what to think. About 2 o'clock they heard trains. Was Johnson leaving or reinforcements coming? It was neither, but a freight train a day late. But an hour later, another train arrived. This one carried the men of Stonewall Jackson. Riding by way of "Rockfish Gap," (Jackson) reached Staunton about 5:00 p.m. and took quarters at the Virginia Hotel.

Monday, May 5, 1862. Jackson remained in Staunton today, getting his hair cut and donning a new suit of Confederate gray. Until this time, he had worn his major's blue uniform from his days at VMI Headquarters were maintained in the Virginia Hotel. The morning was nice, but the afternoon brought rain.

His troops were encamped around Staunton. The Stonewall Brigade was two miles east of town near the local cemetery.

Tuesday, May 6, 1982. This was a fine spring day, and many of the farmers planted corn. Jackson was not planting corn though. From his headquarters at the Virginia Hotel in Staunton, he plotted strategy. Ed Johnson, west of town with 2,800 men, was already skirmishing with units under Milroy.

Wednesday, May 7, 1862. Always seeking to confuse and mistify the enemy, Jackson and part of the staff left Staunton early in the morning. It appeared as though he was headed for Lexington, but then he cut across to the Staunton and Parkersburg Turnpike. Even the remaining staff was confused, they started toward Lexington and then had to double back. His own infantry was being sent to reinforce the 2,800 under Johnson. Leading elements of the two armies engaged in probing actions throughout the day.

Thursday, May 8, 1862. Today, twenty-five miles west of Staunton, the Battle of McDowell took place. Jackson wanted to flank Milroy, but before he was able to do this, Milroy made an assault on Sitlington's Hill which dominated the field. The terrain restricted the number of troops that could be used. Late in the evening General Johnson was wounded. Jackson spoke with him as he was being brought down the mountain in an ambulance. Jackson placed Taliafferro in charge and sent word with Jed Hotchkiss that he was coming in person with the Stonewall Brigade. There was much confusion between 8 and 9 p.m. Jackson came up and talked with General Winder. It was very late when he and the staff started back to Wilson's. The Union army had been repulsed.

Friday, May 9, 1862. It was 2:00 a.m. when Jackson got back to John Wilson's. The house and the yard were full of wounded. Hotchkiss was ordered to go on a scouting expedition after an hour's rest. Frost covered the ground. And Hotchkiss learned that the men in blue had withdrawn. But Jackson's men were too tired to pursue. The Confederate loss was high, and Ed Johnson had a bad leg wound. Rations were cooked and enemy stores gathered up. Local residents were glad the Confederates had punished the enemy. They had been victimized by burnings and harassment. Headquarters was placed at Mrs. Phoenix Hull's in McDowell. Confederate dead were buried at a bend of the road.

Saturday, May 10, 1862. Jackson got an early start in pursuit of the enemy, marching on the Parkersburg road, six miles toward Monterey. Then the column turned northeast toward Franklin. After covering a distance of ten miles, Jackson asked Hotchkiss to see that the roads leading from Franklin into the Valley were blocked. At this point as he sought to keep Fremont from joining Banks, he shared a military jewel with Hotchkiss, "No don't take any counsel of your fears."

Sunday, May 11, 1862. Near Franklin. After the war, Jed learned that Mr. Lincoln had wanted Fremont to use the very road Jackson blockaded in an effort to join Banks at Harrisonburg.

Headquarters at Franklin in a meadow a mile and a half from town.

Monday, May 12, 1862. Near Franklin. Divine services held to thank God for Protection and victory.

Tuesday, May 13, 1862. Headquarters at Solomon Flesher's, "a brick house on the south side of the river ½ mile S.W. from Franklin."

Wednesday, May 14, 1862. Headquarters at the home of Mrs. Felix Hull.

Thursday, May 15, 1862. Jackson traveled to Lebanon and White Sulphur Springs. Quarters were secured at King's. An order was issued to observe May 16 as a fast.

Friday, May 16, 1862. The army remained camped around Lebanon. "Fast Day" was observed at headquarters at King's.

Saturday, May 17, 1862. The army marched at Jackson's "early hour," and then "encamped on the North River opposite Bridgewater, the rear in the vicinity of Mt. Solon." With the advance near Bridgewater, Jackson established headquarters in tents, on Castle Hill, just west of Mt. Solon. The staff dined at the home of Major J.W. McCue. One of the guests was Brig. Gen. George H. Steuart of Maryland.

Sunday, May 18, 1862. Headquarters still at Mt. Solon. Jackson, Jed Hotchkiss, and Major R.L. Dabney rode via Mossy Creek to a point near Bridgewater. There, Major Rev. Dabney preached. Them some of the officers went to the home of George Gibbons for dinner. Their host told them many things about the Yankee occupation of the area. Richard E. Ewell arrived in camp this morning. He rode with Jackson to church, and then back to his command at Conrad's Store.

Monday, May 19, 1862. Jackson had the men up and at breakfast at 2:00 a.m. Nothing like an early breakfast. An hour later, at 3:00 a.m., his columns were under way. The North River was crossed in an unique manner. Wagons donated by the citizens were pushed into the river and planked for a bridge. It was a nice warm day. The advance of the army reached Dayton, while the rear of the column camped near Bridgewater. Headquarters "were in a tent near the old stream mill just below Harrisonburg."

    Hotchkiss and Boswell were sent on a scouting expedition. Meeting Ashby near New Market, after a ride of thirty-six miles, they were told that the main body of enemy troops was at Strasburg. Jed intended to stay at Rev. Rude's but found his daughter was a corpse in the house.

Tuesday, May 20, 1862. Jackson moved to Tenth Legion. The army covered 12 miles heading for New Market. Met General Richard Taylor; complimented him on his troops.[10]

Wednesday, May 21, 1862. On the march, riding with Dick Taylor crossed the Luray Gap. Camp on the other side.

Thursday, May 22, 1862. Today Jackson began his march down through the Luray Valley to Front Royal. Ewell's division was in the lead. Ashby did a lovely job shielding the movements.

Friday, May 23, 1862. Today was the Battle of Front Royal. Ewell's command commenced the action. Belle Boyd ran out of the woods to give helpful information. Jackson charges across the bridge amid the smoke and flame. Taylor's book the best source.

Dick Taylor's command was in the advance. Jackson was riding with him. "The road led north between the east bank of the river and the western base of the Blue Ridge." Rain had fallen and made the rough very bad. "Past midday we reached a wood extending from the mountain to the river, when a mounted officer from the rear called Jackson's attention, who rode back with him. A moment later, there rushed out of the wood to meet us a young, rather well-looking woman." This was Belle Boyd.[11] She was breathless. Regaining her voice, she gave Jackson informatin about the military situation. Belle said Front Royal was filled with Federals. Their camp was located on the west side of the river. They had guns in position to cover the wagon bridge, but none covering the railroad bridge. Banks was at Winchester and thought Jackson was at Harrisonburg. She gave all this information to Jackson with the precision of a staff officer. Supposedly Jackson knew all of this when he was at New Market. But Belle's words certainly confirmed his intelligence.

Jackson's objective was to clear the town of the Federals, and take at least one of the bridges intact so he would have a clear road to Winchester. From this road, the present Route 340, country roads ran westward and intersected witht he Valley Pike. The river was deep, swollen by recent rains, and the current was swift. Therefore, the bridge was of the utmost importance.

Jackson Day By Day

In the streets of Front Royal, the First Maryland Infantry U.S.A., fought the First Maryland C.S.A. The quick strike of the Confederate army prevented the Union men from burning the bridge. Taylor and Jackson galloped through the fire and smoke.

Saturday, May 24, 1862. Basically at Cedarville, south of Winchester on what is today Route 340 leading to Front Royal. Thre was rain and hail in the morning. Ewell and his men went to Nineveh. Jackson and Ewell conferred.

Jackson moved on toward Middletown. Banks was either late in getting intelligence or else did not appreciate his serious predicament. He waited at Strasburg until the last possible moment. Jackson's hope was to cut him in two at Middletown. Poague's battery and a detachment of Ashby's cavalry was sent to do the job. The Confederate attack created havoc. A Union stampede resulted, and vast stores fell into Confederate hands.

Jackson directed some of Poague's fire in person. General Taylor had sent some infantrymen to protect the commander.

Ashby spurred his black stallion and went after some of the Rebels. Many felt he was too reckless. Jackson gave him a mild reprimand.

Jackson, staff and couriers rode on toward Winchester. Once he dismounted and went to an overturned wagon and obtained a cracker. He asked Douglas what he thought of the ladies of Winchester. Without waiting for Henry to reply, the General said, "Don't you think they are a noble set, worth fighting for?....They are the truest people in the South."

After dark, Jackson and his party reached Newtown. He was dismayed to find that Ashby's cavalry had given up their chase to plunder the Union wagons. Jackson never ceased to lament and condemn the failure of the cavalry and the want of discipline at this moment. He felt Banks would have been completely destroyed.

Sunday, May 25, 1862. "Galloping down the hill, the General and staff went into town with the skirmishers, and Winchester - the 'Bandy Ball of the Confederacy'...that day was again in the hands of her friends...

The streets were lined with people....They had come to meet their own troops, who soon forgot their fatigue in the joy of their reception. Windows and doors, closed for months, were thrown open; there were merry voices and bright faces. For a moment, but only for a moment, the dead and wounded on the field seemed forgotten. Then a missing face here and there sent relatives scurrying to the battlefield....

Flames from burning buildings, set on fire by General Banks,...soon began to shoot up wildly into the sky and heavy black smoke threw a pall over the town. Terrible as it looked it only heightened the excitement and enthusiasm of the populace. The reception of General Jackson cannot be described. There were tears and smiles, like rain and sunshine; lips that spoke blessing, and quivering lips that could not speak at all; men, women, and children all joining in the strange welcome. They ignored the sufferings they had gone through and their own fortitude, their losses, their anxieties, but they convinced him surely that they were 'worth fighting for.' "[12]

But Jackson was not satisfied, he wanted to "Push on to the Potomac." When the enemy was on the run, chase him until he gives out.

Monday, May 26, 1862. Winchester. Taylor Hotel. Jackson sends his report to Richmond stating:

"During the last three days, God has blessed our arms with brilliant success. On Friday the Federals at Front Royal were routed and one section of artillery in addition to many prisoners captured. On Saturday Banks' main column while retreating from Strasburg to Winchester was pierced....On Sunday the other part was routed at this place."[13]

Jackson observed the Sabbath a day late. By order of the General, chaplains held services at 4:00 p.m. The army was to "recognize the hand of a Protecting Providence in the brilliant successes of the past three days which have given us the results of a great victory without great losses...."

Jackson also approved the humane act of Dr. Hunter McGuire who released eight Union doctors from captivity on the condition that eight Confederate doctors would be released.[14]

The army rejoiced in its achievements, and in the huge amount of supplies captured from Commissary Banks. Not only had Banks lost one fourth of his command, but the Rebels gathered 9,000 small arms, and 500,000 rounds of ammunition. Cattle, bacon, bread, sugar and salt were also captured.

Tuesday, May 27, 1862. Winchester.

Wednesday, May 28, 1862. Winchester. Winder's brigade along with the batteries of Carpenter and Poague was ordered northward to Harpers Ferry. Jackson directed all available wagons to gather at Martinsburg to help haul the captured supplies.

Winder moved out at 5:00 a.m. A Rebel cavalryman met Winder enroute to Charlestown and told him the Yankees were entrenching south and west of the town. Winder sent the message back to Jackson and kept on going.

A mile from Charlestown, Winder met the Yankees and drove them back, brushing them aside easily. People lined the streets to welcome the Confederate troops. Four miles beyond the town, Winder halted. Large numbers of Union troops could be seen on Bolivar Heights.

Meanwhile Jackson was informed by an elderly man that Union forces were moving on Front Royal.

Thursday, May 29, 1862. Jackson arrived with the Second Virginia and met with Winder. A detachment was sent to dislodge the Yankees from Loudoun Heights. The rest of the army camped at Halltown. But the situation was deteriorating. Ashby confirmed the earlier report. Fremont was moving toward Strasburg in an effort to unite with Shields. This was trouble, a pincers.

Friday, May 30, 1862. This morning messengers came to Jackson's headquarters in Charlestown with news of a new Union threat, stating Union forces were regrouping and that General Shields was headed toward Front Royal. Ladies of the town came to pay their tribute to Jackson. Some of the troops bathed in the Shenandoah River, and most of the staff ate at the home of Major W.J. Hawks. Late in the day, the commander took the train back to Winchester.[15]

Saturday, May 31, 1862. The next three weeks were to produce long and sleepless days and nights for Jackson. Many feel this contributed to his seemingly lack of effort later on the peninsula. At 3:00 a.m. the General roused Hotchkiss and asked him to go to Charlestown and bring back the troops to meet the rumored Yankee threat. About 2:30 p.m., Jackson left Winchester and headed for Strasburg. The trip from Harpers Ferry to Winchester and then south marked the final ten days of the Valley campaign. The weather was hot and humid, with heavy rains, long marches, constant threats from the Union and continual skirmishes, and all the time, Jackson had to worry with large trains.

Sunday, June 1, 1862. Jackson started the day at Hupp's, a mile from Strasburg. Lively action commenced about noon and Jackson deployed his troops over the hills northwest of Woodstock. Hotchkiss was sent to Round Hill to observe.

Monday, June 2, 1862. Jackson was busy supervising deployment against Fremont and the tangle of his supply trains. No train was allowed to stop or water. They had to keep moving. There was a heavy shower in the afternoon. Jackson reached Israel Allen's near Hawkinstown. Rain and hail followed the main column to Woodstock. It was almost midnight before they arrived.

Tuesday, June 3, 1862. Rain for the third straight day made life miserable for Jackson. Camp was made in Dr. Rice's field below New Market. The staff was upset because Jackson refused the offer to stay in a home. Jackson may have regretted the decision also. During the night a small river ran through his tent and swept his belongings into the field.

Wednesday, June 4, 1862. Rain continued to plague the army. The tents were flooded during the night, so the general and his staff took shelter in the home of Mr. Strayer. Twice during the day, Jackson conferred with Hotchkiss about the terrain around Port Republic. Jackson was wet and weary.[16] He was interviewed by a Union correspondent.

Thursday, June 5, 1862. Passing through Harrisonburg. Jackson moved on the Port Republic Road. Ewell was nearby.

Friday, June 6, 1862. Confederate cavalry and infantry engaged Yankee troops on the Port Republic Road near Harrisonburg. Turner Ashby sought to cut off the Union line of retreat, and in doing so was killed. Jackson was at Dr. Kemper's at Port Republic when he got the news. Jackson was deeply touched and walked the floor of his room alone in his sorrow. Port Republic is a small village situated at the junction of the Middle Branch and South Branch as they flow together to form the South Fork of the Shenandoah.

Saturday, June 7, 1862. Jackson offered battle near Cross Keys, but the Union forces did not advance.

Sunday, June 8, 1862. Jackson and his staff barely escaped capture this morning. While crossing the North River, they were surprised by Yankee cavalry. This was one time that he was surprised. Headquarters was struck. Jackson berated Dr. Hunter McGuire for cursing the horses while evacuating wounded from a church.

While Jackson was having his problems, Richard S. Ewell met John Fremont's columns at Cross Keys, approximately six miles from Harrisonburg. It was a long and bloody conflict, but night brought a Confederate victory. Ewell was left to resist Fremont should he try again tomorrow. The rest of the army headed for Port Republic, "which lies in the forks of the river," and made his arrangements to attack the troops of Shields' command next morning on the Lewis farm, just below the town.[17]

John Imboden had held the bridge across North River at Mount Crawford while the fighting raged at Cross Keys. His second assignment was to prevent Union cavalry from attacking Jackson's trains at Port Republic. About 10:00 p.m. Imboden received a note from Jackson. It was written on the blank margin of a newspaper, directing him to come to Port Republic. Jackson also added the note, "poor Ashby is dead. He fell gloriously...I know you will join me in mourning the loss of our friend, one of the noblest men and soldiers in the Confederate army."[18] Imboden carried that paper until it wore out.

Monday, June 9, 1862. Imboden reached Port Republic an hour before dawn. He found the house where Jackson was staying. Not wishing to disturb the commander, John asked where Sandie Pendleton was staying.

"Upstairs, first room on the right was the reply."

Bounding up the steps, Imboden entered the wrong room and entered Jackson's room. The General was "lying on his face across the bed, fully dressed with sword, sash and boots all on. The low-burnt tallow candle on the table shed a dim light, yet enough by which to recognize him. I endeavored to withdraw without waking him. He turned over, sat up on the bed, and called out, 'Who is that?' "

He checked Imboden's apology with, "That is all right. It's time to be up. I am glad to see you. Were the men all up when you came through the camp?"

Imboden replied that they were. He asked his cavalry leader to sit down, saying he wanted to talk with him. Subordinates knew not to ask questions. Jackson paused and then spoke "very feelingly to Ashby's death."

Imboden said he had done great things in the last four weeks. To this Jackson replied, "Yes, God blessed our army again yesterday, and I hope with his protection and blessing we shall do still better today."[19]

Monday, June 9, 1862. Today was the battle of Cross Keys.[20] Another victory.

From the time of Jackson's arrival in Staunton until the battle of Port Republic, thirty-five days passed. In that time, he "marched from Staunton to McDowell, 40 miles; from McDowell to Front Royal, about 110; from Front Royal to Winchester, 20 miles; Winchester to Port Republic, 75 miles; a total of 245 miles, fighting in the meantime 4 desperate battles and winning them all."

"Jackson's military operations were always unexpected and mysterious." Early in the war he told John Imboden, "There are two things never to be lost sight of by a military commander, always mystify, mislead, and surprise the enemy if possible; and when you strike and overcome him, never let up in your pursuit so long as your men have strength to follow; for an army routed, if hotly pursued, becomes panic stricken and can then be destroyed by half their number. The other rule is never fight against heavy odds, if by any possible manuevering you can hurl your own force on only a part, and the weakest part, of your enemy and crush it. Such tactics will win every time, and a small army may thus destroy a large one in detail, and repeated victory will make it invincible."

"His celerity of movement was a simple matter. He never broke down his men by too-long continued marching. He rested the whole column very often, but only for a few minutes at a time. I remember that he liked to see the men lie down flat on the ground to rest and would say, 'A man rests all over when he lies down.' "[21]

These words by Imboden describe to the letter Jackson in the Valley and throughout the war.

VI
THE SUMMER OF 1862

While Jackson was striking fear into the hearts of the Union leaders in Washington and tying up 60,000 men under Fremont, Banks, and Shields, George B. McClellan was massing a large army on the Peninsula for a drive on Richmond. The result was the Seven Days Campaign with action south and east of Richmond.

McClellan transported his army via boat down the Potomac and across the Chesapeake Bay to Fort Monroe. He planned to thrust inland between the York and the James rivers. It was an extensive operation.

Confederate defenses were brushed aside at Yorktown and Williamsburg. However, heroic action at Drewry's Bluff turned back Federal gunboats. By the 15th of May, five Federal Corps encircled Richmond to the north and east. They were just six miles away. But Jackson's actions in the Shenandoah Valley kept McDowell from coming to join McClellan. Lincoln feared for the safety of Washington.

The Confederates, hoping to stem the tide launched a savage attack at Seven Pines or Fair Oaks. General Joseph E. Johnston was severely wounded and Robert E. Lee took command of the army.

Lee began the work which brought him the name, "The King of Spades." He built entrenchments around the city of Richmond, and also planned for a counter offensive.

On June 25 the Seven Days action began with fighting the next several days at Beaver Dam, Gaines' Mill, Savage Station and Glendale or Frayer's Farm. Confederates tried to storm Malvern Hill, but suffered heavy losses. McClellan had had enough and withdrew during the night to Harrison's Landing. Union Losses were 15,849; Confederate 20,614.

In mid-June, Jackson was miles away to the west. We turn now to the story of how he joined Lee, and his role in the Seven Days action.

Tuesday, June 10, 1862. It rained most of the day. Some felt that Jackson had done poorly. The command suffered what they considered to be heavy losses. Headquarters was at the home of John F. Lewis at Mount Vernon Furnace.

Wednesday, June 11, 1862. Jackson had Hotchkiss and his staff busy checking the fords and the conditions of the roads. The General had the idea of using the infantry to throw stones into the ford to make it more shallow. The nice day was spent at the Lewis home.

Thursday, June 12, 1862. Jackson and his men left the Lewis home early in the morning. The General went to Port Republic to watch the troops cross the river.

Friday, June 13, 1862. The command was encamped between Middle and South Rivers, near Weyer's Cave. The men and their commander needed rest. Jackson ordered the men to wash and clean up. Jackson invited his command, "to observe tomorrow evening, June 14 from 3 o'clock p.m., as a season of thanksgiving, by a suspension of all military exercises and by holding divine service in the several regiments...for the purpose of rendering thanks to God for having crowned our arms with success and to implore his continued favor."

Saturday, June 14, 1862. The Day of Thanksgiving and Prayer Camp was still in the corner of the woods at the point Weyer's Cave Road left the Port Republic Road.

Sunday, June 15, 1862. Services were held in the various camps. Jackson heard Rev. Dabney. And later in the day went to Holy Communion at the Third Brigade camp site. "It was a very impressive celebration of the Lord's Supper, in the woods amid the din of camp hushed for a brief period to celebrate the Supper of the Prince of Peace. The General attended the meeting, humbly devout."

Monday, June 16, 1862. Today Jackson met with General Whiting. Some thought the command would be heading back to Winchester. Jackson gave the command that the men should move "at early dawn," a favorite phrase. After dark, Jackson headed toward Staunton, but turned and went to Mount Crawford to hold a secret meeting with Col. Munford, telling him how to follow and harass Fremont and the Union forces. (Hotchkiss says this was the 17th).

Today General Lee wrote to Jackson saying that McClellan was being reinforced. Lee felt they would have to make a united front and said "if you agree with me, move on Richmond, the sooner the better."

Tuesday, June 17, 1862. Mount Meridan.

Wednesday, June 18, 1862. About 5:00 p.m. Jackson arrived in Waynesboro. He told no one anything but shook hands and put his trunk on the train. When asked what he was up to, he said "Can you keep a secret? Yes? Ah, so can I." He conferred with General Whiting at the foot of the mountain and sent off some telegraph messages. The whole army was moving, but no one except Jackson seemed to know where. Lodging was found at the home of James McCue on the east side of the Blue Ridge. Jackson prayed for a long time before retiring. Sleeping in the same room with the commander, Hotchkiss told him comments about the destination of the column. After listening to his map maker, Jackson said, "Do any of them say I am going to Washington?"

Thursday, June 19, 1862. Jackson, Jed and others rode toward Mechum's River. Jackson was in good spirits and talkative.

Friday, June 20, 1862. The command was delayed in Gordonsville today by a Union threat and also by slow progress. Jackson was in a comfortable home for awhile.

Saturday, June 21, 1862. Today, the General moved his men "rapidly down the Virginia Central Railway on ten trains of eighteen to twenty freight cars each." Spent the night at Fredericks Hall.

Sunday, June 22, 1862. Jackson arrived at Fredericks Hall ahead of his men and spent the day attending religious services. Early in the evening he went to his room at the home of Nat Harris. He would wait until the Sabbath ended and then fulfill the request in Lee's letter of the 16th, "I'd like to confer with you at some point on your approach to the Chickahominy."

Monday, June 23, 1862. This had to be one of the biggest days in Jackson's life, one which shows his rugged constitution, devotion to duty, and commitment to the cause. Mounting up and leaving the Harris home with just one attendant, Charles Harris, Jackson rode much like the pony express riders. In fourteen hours he covered fifty-two miles, a remarkable feat, and arrived at Lee's headquarters at the Dabbs home about 3:00 p.m. He was covered with dust and had to be a little stiff. Lee was in conference so Jackson did not go inside immediately. Instead, he talked with his brother-in-law, D.H. Hill in the yard. Harris held the reins of the sweating, panting horse. Lee was amazed and gave Jackson a glass of milk. That must have been the only nourishment Tom had all day. Then Lee, Longstreet, A.P. Hill, and Jackson conferred. When they were finished, Jackson mounted up for his return trip of over fifty miles, rejoining his lead elements after midnight.

Tuesday, June 24, 1862. A brief rest was all that Jackson took after the long, exhaustive ride. He was up before dawn and on the road with his troops heading toward Ashland.[1]

Wednesday, June 25, 1862. Again on the march toward Ashland. Major Jasper Whiting, a man familiar with the terrain of the area reported to Jackson. Things were not good. 18,500 troops were spread over fifteen miles of road. The men were hampered by the mud, heat and showers. It was far different from marching in the Shenandoah Valley.

Thursday, June 26, 1862. Jackson had been in prayer early in the morning. Then after giving orders to his lieutenants, the men marched from Ashland to Huntley's Corners.

Friday, June 27, 1862. Lee and Jackson talked at Walnut Grove Church, two miles east of Elkerson's Mill. Jackson had been in prayer in the early morning hours and had given orders to his lieutenants. The troops covered the distance from Huntley's Corners to Old Cold Harbor. Today was the battle of Gaines Mill.

Saturday, June 28, 1862. Conferred with Jeb Stuart in early a.m. near Gaines Mills.

Sunday, June 29, 1862. Rebuilt Grapevine Bridge, and prepared to pursue retreating Federals. Near Gaines Mills.

Monday, June 30, 1862. Jackson was awakened by rain about 1:00 a.m. He talked with General Magruder at 3:30. He seemed numb with exhaustion, very weary. Lee joined the two generals. Daylight brought one of the mysteries of Jackson's career, why didn't he cross the Grapevine Bridge earlier and carry out his assignment? "A strange inertia seemed to overwhelm Jackson." He may have thought the Federals were too strongly intrenched, or he may have been too tired to think straight, or a combination of both. Dr. Freeman says that "Frayser Farm was one of the great lost opportunities of Confederate military history. It was the bitterest disappointment Lee ever sustained. Never again was he to have such a golden opportunity."[1]

Thus ended the month of June for Jackson. It had taken its toll on Jackson, physically and mentally. It had been one of the worst Jackson had faced in terms of travel and the loss of sleep. We have already referred to the first days in June. The first ten were involved in the ending of the Valley Campaign. The second ten were spent in traveling from the Shenandoah to the Richmond area. Then from June 22-30 Jackson rode over a hundred miles in a day, lost several nights sleep, and when he did get to sleep was at the edge of a battlefield, up at dawn, traveling, and making decisions. He was so tired he went to sleep with a biscuit in his mouth.

Tuesday, July 1, 1862. Malvern Hill.

Wednesday, July 2, 1862. On this rainy morning, Lee confers with Jackson and Longstreet at the Poindexter farmhouse. They study maps and ask "Where has McClellan gone?" President Jefferson Davis arrived with his brother. Davis and Lee plan strategy without consulting Jackson.

Thursday, July 3, 1862. The Confederates tried to converge on Malvern Hill. Longstreet was in the lead, perhaps due to Jackson's poor showing. The pace was slow and the roads rough. This made Jackson irritable. By nightfall, a house was selected for headquarters, "a mile or two east of Willis Church." He told the staff to be up at dawn.

Friday, July 4, 1862. Jackson was in poor spirits this morning. Only Major Dabney was up at the appointed hour. The General vented his rage on him. Jim scattered the breakfast and poured the coffee on the ground. The command marched to a position near Harrison's Landing. Jackson did not want to attack. He and Lee rode forward to look the situation over.

Saturday, July 5, 1862. Near Westover.

Sunday, July 6, 1862. Near Westover.

Monday, July 7, 1862. Near Westover. "Approximately three miles north of the James River and twenty-five miles below Richmond. Jackson was not feeling well.

Tuesday, July 8, 1862. Near Westover. Orders came to move to Richmond.

Wednesday, July 9, 1862. Leaving for Richmond. The command

marched up the peninsula and into camp on the Mechanicsville Turnpike.

Thursday, July 10, 1862. Three miles from Richmond at Glenwood, the farm of Hugh A. White, a nephew of William Poague of the Rockbridge Artillery.

Friday, July 11, 1862. Near Richmond.

Saturday, July 12, 1862. Near Richmond.

Sunday, July 13, 1862. Jackson made his first public appearance since his rise to fame in Richmond. He attended services at Second Presbyterian Church where his friend, Dr. Moses D. Hoge was preaching.[2] He slipped into the church quietly, and apparently left before folks could gather around him at the close. The U.D.C. have placed a marker in the church.

According to Rev. Dabney and Mrs. Jackson, the General took time to visit a mother whose son had been killed in action. He also conferred with President Davis at the White House of the Confederacy. Lee was also there. Jackson gave Hoge a pass to travel anywhere in his command, and in the afternoon, the famous preacher spoke at the encampment of the "Stonewall Brigade." Jackson attended that service also.

Monday, July 14, 1862. Jackson writes to his wife describing his Sabbath. He was happy to be once again in the house of God.

Tuesday, July 15, 1862. Heading west from Richmond.

Wednesday, July 16, 1862. Heading westward.

Thursday, July 17, 1862. Moving toward Fredericks Hall.

Friday, July 18, 1862. Headquarters at Harris' Fredericks Hall. This is twenty-six miles from Gordonsville on the Virginia Central Railroad.

Saturday, July 19, 1862. Jackson arrived in Gordonsville today. Jed Hotchkiss noticed that he looked bad from his experiences on the peninsula as did the troops. The General looked weary to his old friends. Jackson put his men in camps around Gordonsville and Louisa Court House. People flocked to see the famous general. On the way to Richmond he had stayed at the home of the Ewings. Now once again he accepted their hospitality. His tent was pitched in the yard, and he wrote to

Anna, "my tent opens upon the Blue Ridge in the distance." The Ewings reminded him of the Grahams back in Winchester. He enjoyed their children, especially a little girl. He promised to give her a button. This was sent months later. Jackson delighted in hearing Mr. Ewing's[3] sermons, and the minister was stirred by Jackson's prayers. Never had he heard anyone pray like Jackson.

Sunday, July 20, 1862. Gordonsville. Jackson went to church today and heard Mr. Ewing preach on "the Goodness and severity of God." Again, he looked weary.

Monday, July 21, 1862. Headquarters established today about four miles from Gordonsville. The entire army picked blackberries. The General ate his share and seemed to enjoy them very much.

Tuesday, July 22, 1862. Gordonsville.

Wednesday, July 23, 1862. Gordonsville.

Thursday, July 24, 1862. Gordonsville.

Friday, July 25, 1862. Gordonsville.

Saturday, July 26, 1862. Gordonsville.

Sunday, July 27, 1862. Gordonsville.

Monday, July 28, 1862. Gordonsville.

Tuesday, July 29, 1862. Gordonsville.

Wednesday, July 30, 1862. Gordonsville.

Thursday, July 31, 1862. Gordonsville.

——————— August 1862 ———————

After McClellan's failure on the peninsula, the scene of action came northward again. This month found Jackson in action at Cedar Mountain and at Second Manassas.

Lincoln not only had troubles with the Confederates, but with his own commanders. John Pope was ordered from the west to form a new army out of the units manhandled by Jackson in the Valley. From the scattered units of Fremont, Banks and McDowell, Pope formed the Army of Virginia.

Pope was an energetic man. He was quite boastful and talked about having headquarters in the saddle. He also said he was used to seeing only the fleeing backs of his enemies. He made stern announcements about what would happen to civilians or guerrillas harassing his troops. His statements brought anger and bitterness to the South.

McClellan on the James and Pope on the Rappahannock had twice as many men as Lee, but they disliked and distrusted each other.

Once again the Confederate strategy was to keep the two commands apart. Working against Pope seemed to be the most logical choice. So as we have seen, Jackson was sent with 12,000 men to Gordonsville. This was key point to hold against and advance from either the North or the South.

Learning that Pope had two divisions near Culpeper, Jackson headed for the area on August 5. Four days later he met them in battle along a little stream near a hill known as Cedar Mountain. Jackson had to bring up A.P. Hill in order to win a victory, and lost General Winder; but he defeated Banks, raising Confederate morale.

On August 13, Lee sent James Longstreet and 25,000 men to Gordonsville. Two days later he left for the town. Less than 25,000 men were left to man the defenses of Richmond. But McClellan did nothing. McClellan still believed that Lee had 200,000 men and that reinforcements were pouring into Richmond daily. George was gloomy. Yet when Pope met with disaster at Second Manassas, he almost rejoiced. He did nothing to help Pope, and wrote to his wife, "I believe I have triumphed! Just received a telegram from Halleck stating that Pope and Burnside are hard pressed."

They were. Pope had about 55,000 men, including 8,000 from Burnside's Corps on the Rapidan. He expected McClellan to join him and perhaps Halleck would arrive from Washington to take overall command.

But this was not to be. Besides, the Rappahannock River was behind him. By forced marching the Confederates could get behind him, cutting off his supplies and also his escape. Lee just missed doing this very thing. Stuart's cavalry missed "an assignment" and Robert Toombs left a river crossing unguarded. And a few days later Pope was joined by elements of the Fifth and Third Corps. In another week Lee would be hopelessly outnumbered.

Now was the time to strike. So Jackson was sent behind the Bull Run Mountains to head east then through Thoroughfare Gap to strike Pope in the rear. Meanwhile, Longstreet would maintain his front. Jackson began his flank movement on August 25. Pope thought he was heading for the Valley. Jackson covered fifty miles in forty hours and swiftly cut Pope off from his supplies. However, he was in difficulty himself. He did not want to withdraw, even strategically. So he decided to stay, destroy Pope's supplies and pin his adversary down until Longstreet came up.

Friday, August 1, 1862. Near Gordonsville.

Saturday, August 2, 1862. Near Gordonsville.

Sunday, August 3, 1862. Jackson and Jed Hotchkiss went to church services in the camp of Lawton's Brigade of Georgia troops. Dr. Stiles preached on "Show Thyself A Man." The chaplain prayed that there would be no straggling in the next action, and that the Lord would give them a big victory. Returning to camp, Jackson had a visitor, the Hon. William C. Rives who pointed out that Lafayette had passed through the area years before.

Monday, August 4, 1862. A quiet day.

Tuesday, August 5, 1862. On this warm day, corps headquarters was moved to Col. Magruders, four miles beyond Gordonsville.

Wednesday, August 6, 1862. The trial of Brig. Gen. Richard B. Garnett, for his actions at Kernstown, was held at Gen. Ewell's headquarters.

Thursday, August 7, 1862. The entire army was on the move today. Jackson slept part of the night on a "stile" in the street of Orange Court House. Later he went to the home of a Mr. Willis.

Friday, August 8, 1862. Action along Cedar Run and at Crooked Run Church. Yankee cavalry was routed. Local citizens complained of the actions of Pope's army. The men in blue had destroyed homes, taken horses, chickens and many

John W. Schildt   69

other items. Pope had ordered his army to subsist on the country.

Saturday, August 9, 1862. Jackson saw the opportunity to strike the Union forces and destroy one Union command and then the other like he had done at Cross Keys and Port Republic. But he did not keep Ewell, Winder and A.P. Hill informed as to his plans. Banks hit hard in the morning and things were bad for Jackson, Winder was not in good health. A.P. Hill came up and saved the day. "The General and his whole staff were exposed to the hottest of fire and all were busy trying to rally the left wing after it fell back..." He personally led some of the men back into the action. Winder fell, shot through the chest. Yankee prisoners cheered Jackson as he rode by. The command slept under the trees.

Sunday, August 10, 1862. Jackson's command occupied the same ground as Saturday during the day. They collected arms, took the wounded to shelter and buried the dead. Union forces were drawn up in line of battle several miles away but did no fighting. The suffering of the wounded men in blue left on the field was terrible. During a wild rumor there was a panic in the wagon train. Jackson himself had to restore order and take steps to see that it did not happen again.

Monday, August 11, 1862. Part of the Army, including Jackson, started for Orange Court House. Jackson came back to Garnett's, took supper and spent the night. Union forces sent a flag of truce to the battlefield to gather their wounded and collect the dead. Stuart and some comrades from days gone by chatted.

Tuesday, August 12, 1862. Camp was made near Toddsburg, near Dr. Pannill's. There was a heavy rain today. Jackson told Hotchkiss to make as many maps as possible from their present location to the Potomac River.

Wednesday, August 13, 1862. In Headquarters planning. James Longstreet came to Gordonsville today.

Thursday, August 14, 1862. Robert E. Lee arrived two-and-a-half miles from Gordonsville on the Madison Turnpike. Jackson went to see him.

Friday, August 15, 1862. Near Gordonsville. More troops arriving all the time. The men think they are headed for Maryland.

Saturday, August 16, 1862. The Second Corps was under way today, marching from Dr. Pannill's to Mountain Run along the southern sope of "Clark's Mountain" six miles from Orange Court House. Headquarters was at Mr. Gymes', four miles from the court house. Col. French of Governor Letcher's staff arrived today.

Sunday, August 17, 1862. Jackson very naturally went to church today on the southern slope of Clark's Mountain. Rev. Tebbs spoke. On the way to services, Jackson talked about what he thought a man ought to be: "always striving to do his duty and never satisfied if anything can be done better." Perhaps this was the secret of his success. Returning from church, the men in Gen. R.A. Pryor's Brigade cheered Jackson.

Monday, August 18, 1862. Jackson moved to Mountain Run today. Headquarters "was opposite the churches on the south side of the Run," on the Crenshaw farm. General Lee was close by. A detainment force had been left to protect Richmond, and now the bulk of the army was moving against John Pope.

Tuesday, August 19, 1862. Orders were "issued to cook three day's rations and be ready to move at moon rising." In the afternoon some men who were found guilty of desertion were lined up and shot. Most of the Second Corps was drawn up to see the shooting.

Wednesday, August 20, 1862. Jackson left the Crenshaw farm on Mountain Run, six miles from Orange Court House at 3:00 a.m. He believed in early starts and marching in the dark to cover his approach. Finding A.P. Hill had not moved out, the General became quite angry. This led to a rift which lasted quite a while and caused a lot of trouble. Jackson had a lot of difficulty in his relationships with general officers. The army then crossed the Rapidan at Somerville Ford and marched to Stevensburg, nine miles from the river. There was a cavalry skirmish at Brandy Station. A halt was made at Jones's Run, two miles beyond Stevensburg. The staff went to bed in a corner of a woods without any supper.

Thursday, August 21, 1862. Once again Jackson and his men started early. No one slept late in Jackson's command. A brief stop was made at Stuart's headquarters at Major Barbour's and military matters were discussed over a good breakfast. Then it was on to the Rappahannock via Brandy Station and Pottsville. The Yankees were posted on the river bank. The Confederates moved in a large body of infantry and support. Jackson's men crossed at Beverly Ford. Jed Hotchkiss says, "Our troops rapidly concentrating and we are engaging the enemy's attention at every ford on the river as we progress...." Jackson spent the night at Mr. Thompson's near St. James Church. "The General was very weary" and enjoyed the glass of milk Jed gave to him. It rained during the night.

Friday, August 22, 1862. Jackson's men moved to Wellford Ford and crossed the Hazel River, fighting the Yankees as they did so. Jackson spent the night near Lee's Springs at a yellow house.

Saturday, August 23, 1862. Jackson remained at Lee's Springs all day. Stuart returned from a triumph raid on Catlet's Station. He captured wagons, prisoners, money, and even important dispatches addressed to Pope himself. The bragging general from the west was up against a different type opponent in the east.

Sunday, August 24, 1862. No permanent bridges had been placed across the river, so the stream had to be recrossed. Jackson was in a bad humor about this and about the lack of food supplies for the men. Camp near Jeffersonton.

Monday, August 25, 1862. Broke camp early near Jeffersonton, tramped to Amissville, and then headed for a ford. It was warm. Jackson advanced to Salem in Fauquier County. Headquarters were made there for the night.

Tuesday, August 26, 1862. Jackson went from Salem by Thoroughfare Gap and Haymarket to Gainesville. He was in position by 4:00 p.m. Stuart joined him. An attack was made on Bristoe Station. Enemy stores were destroyed.

Wednesday, August 27, 1862. Things in place for the Second Battle of Manassas. Jackson hit Manassas Junction at daylight. Many stores and much equipment captured. Jackson reached Manassas at noon. Headquarters made there while part of the army moved off toward Centreville. 50,000 pounds of bacon, 1,000 barrels of corned beef, 2,000 barrels of salt pork, and 2,000 barrels of flour were captured. Flames lit the sky at night as all that could not be carried off was destroyed.

Thursday, August 28, 1862. The Stonewall Brigade was on a high ridge near Groveton, near the Henry House Hill. It was a hot day. The men waited for action most of the day. At 5:00 p.m. it came. The Stonewall Brigade collided with the Union Iron Brigade under John Gibbon. It was a classic struggle. Col. Botts of the Second Virginia was mortally wounded, and Colonel John Neff,[4] the twenty-eight-year-old commander of the 33rd Virginia was killed. It was a blood-smeared field. When the action was finished the Twenty-seventh Virginia had but twenty-five men. Jackson and Stuart spent the night near Sudley Mills. During the night, Jackson moved his lines to the left of the Groveton battlefield. Jackson posted his men near the railroad cut of the unfinished spur of the Manassas Gap Railroad.

Friday, August 29, 1862. This morning the Second Battle of Manassas begain in earnest. Longstreet came up. Others have told the story of the battle, so we will not go into that here. When night came Col. Baylor, commanding the Stonewall Brigade and Captain Hugh White of The Second Virginia, found Chaplain Abner Hopkins and urged a prayer meeting to thank God for preserving their lives. Soon many men were gathered to pray.

Saturday, August 30, 1862. Jackson had his headquarters near Sudley Church. He directed his men as they withstood strong Union attacks along the line of the unfinished railroad cut. Wave after wave came forward. Gallant men met brave men. Colonel Baylor grabbed the colors of the Thirty-third Virginia and was shot down. Captain White seized the flag. He took a step and was riddled by several bullets. The prayer meeting of the previous evening had helped them to prepare for eternity. Hugh was the son of Dr. William White, Jackson's pastor. The Stonewall Brigade lost 415 men out of 635 engaged.

Sunday, August 31, 1862. It poured down rain today, perhaps washing the earth of the bloodshed. Union and Confederates alike gathered and buried their dead and treated their wounded. Jackson moved toward Pleasant Valley and Chantilly.

VII
THE MARYLAND
CAMPAIGN

Lee and Jackson had been victorious. The threat to Richmond had been removed. John Pope had been defeated. Now seemed like a good time to carry the war into the North. The farmers of Virginia needed time to recover from the ravages of war, and to harvest the crops that remained. Perhaps, recruits could be obtained in Maryland, and a victory north of the river might bring Maryland into the Confederacy. Also, a victory on Maryland soil could possibly win recognition of the Confederacy by England and France, and thus foreshadow Southern Independence. The stakes were high, and the invasion was worth the risk. So it was off to Maryland.[1]

Monday, September 1, 1862. Headquarters was established at a small house in Pleasant Valley. Jackson and Hotchkiss had a bite to eat. The General asked for some maps. Then he headed for Chantilly. It was a very stormy day. Other elements of the army clashed with the Federals at Chantilly, and Generals Kearney and Stevens were killed. The night became quite cold. Jackson made his headquarters at an old house a little beyond Chantilly.

Tuesday, September 2, 1862. A clear cool day. The troops tried to dry out.

Wednesday, September 3, 1862. The command traveled by "the Ox Road" to Dranesville.

Thursday, September 4, 1862. The citizens of Leesburg welcomed the Confederate army. Jackson's command camped north of town along the current U.S. 15 getting ready to cross the Potomac.

Friday, September 5, 1862. This was another big day in the life of Jackson. His command, along with the rest of the Army of Northern Virginia, crossed the Potomac River at White's Ford. It was a gala time. The banners waved and the bands played.[2] The soldiers cheered Jackson as he rode through their midst. A boat load of mellons were captured on the Chesapeake and

Ohio Canal. Jackson and his staff sampled them. Then the column headed for Buckeystown in Frederick County. One very friendly Marylander gave Jackson a new horse. The General ordered a field of corn to be purchased along with rails. Roasting ears were to be prepared so the men would have one day of rations. Camp was made at Three Springs, six miles from Frederick.

Saturday, September 6, 1982. Today Confederate troops occupied Frederick, Maryland. Some stores were captured. Jackson ate an ear of corn as an example to his troops. The horse given the General by a Marylander threw him and bruised him. Camp was made south of Frederick in Best's Grove, near where the current Francis Scott Key Shopping Mall is located. A marker can be found on Maryland Route 355. The Monocacy River and the B and O Railroad were just south of the bivouac area.

Sunday, September 7, 1862. In camp south of Frederick at Best's Grove. Visited by some adoring ladies who wanted autographs and buttons. The mother of Henry Kyd Douglas journeyed to headquarters from Shepherdstown and was introduced to the general by her son. Later in the day, Jackson secured a pass and rode into Frederick to attend services at the German Reformed Church. He fell asleep and did not hear the preacher pray for Mr. Lincoln.[3] A very warm September Sunday.

Monday, September 8, 1862. Still in camp south of Frederick. Today Jackson studied maps and asked about the roads to Pennsylvania. He also wrote to Mrs. Jackson describing the beauty of Frederick, and lamenting the fact that he had fallen asleep in church. He also asked James P. Smith, a divinity student, to join his staff.

Tuesday, September 9, 1862. Today, Jackson made his preparations for the movement against Harpers Ferry. Many people came from Frederick to take a look at Jackson. A warm day.

Wednesday, September 10, 1862. Early this morning, all elements of the Army of Northern Virginia broke camp south of Frederick. Jackson and his command joined the march in compliance with Order No. 191 (this was Lee's plan to capture Harpers Ferry). Jackson rode into West Second Street in an effort to see an old friend, Rev. Ross, a Presbyterian pastor. But the cleric was asleep. Jackson then waved, rejoined his command west of the Barbara Fritchie house. Thus he did not see the old lady. Little girls waved their Union flags at him as he passed through Middletown. He tells Douglas, "Evidently, we have no friends in this town."[4] The General is almost captured by Union cavalry on the western slope of South Mountain. He loses his glove as he gallops back to the safety of his command. Camp is made on the farm of John Murdock. While riding, he conversed with Chaplain Hopkins about the state of Col. Baylor's soul.

Thursday, September 11, 1862. Leaving the western slopes of South Mountain, Jackson and his men continued west on the National Road (now alternate 40) passing through Boonsboro and then turning "Column South," or left on what is now Maryland 68. Taking the picturesque country road, the command reached Williamsport, and there forded the Potomac. Once again Jackson saw his first Civil War battlefield, Falling Waters. The men continued to march to Hammond's Mill, a mile and a half from the North Mountain Depot on the B and O Railroad. Jackson made his headquarters at Hammond's Mill. It was a warm day with showers in the evening.

Friday, September 12, 1862. Jackson went by way of Hedgesville and captured Martinsburg. The General was stormed not by Union troops, but by young ladies seeking buttons from his coat. Some even wanted a lock of his hair. But that was going too far. Failing to obtain his hair, they cut off the tail of his horse. Camp was made in a field five miles from Martinsburg. On this pleasant day, Jed Hotchkiss obtained a new hat for his commander.

Saturday, September 13, 1862. On this warm Saturday, Jackson moved closer to Harpers Ferry and his eventual position on Bolivar Heights. Jed Hotchkiss was ordered to open signal communications with other Confederate units on Maryland and Loudon Heights.

Sunday, September 14, 1862. Jackson was the lone bright spot in Lee's army today. Union attacks forced Lee from the South Mountain passes, and the day went against him. He sent word to Jackson to join him as quickly as possible around Sharpsburg. However, "Stonewall" spent the day getting his forces into position for the assault on Harpers Ferry.

Monday, September 15, 1862. With the misty dawn, Jackson opened a heavy fire on Harpers Ferry. Shells rained on the town and the Union garrison from Maryland, Loudoun, and Bolivar Heights. The cannon had zeroed in on Sunday. In about an hour A.P. Hill's infantry was ordered forward. Soon a white flag was seen. And Jackson received the unconditional surrender. It was a big victory; 11,000 prisoners, 12,000 arms, 70 pieces of artillery, and many other supplies. Jackson sent a note to Lee saying, "Through God's blessing Harpers Ferry and its garrison are to surrendered." A.P. Hill was left to take care of the details, and Jackson set the rest of his command in motion for the fields around Sharpsburg. By nightfall, the General was close to the Shepherdstown ford.

Tuesday, September 16, 1862. This morning Jackson reported to Lee at Sharpsburg, and the Confederate commander breathed a sigh of relief. His men had moved at a pace more gruelling than the Valley Campaign. "In three and a half days they had covered over sixty miles....The weather had been intensely hot and the dust was terrible." Jackson made his headquarters at the farm of David Smith at the west edge of Sharpsburg, and made troop dispositions.

Wednesday, September 17, 1862. America's bloodiest day. Jackson was up early and directed his troops around the Dunker Church and the West Woods. He took and inflicted heavy losses. Dr. McGuire gave him one of his favorite lemons, and he told the Winchester physician, "I fear they have done their worst." Yet he had staff officers scout the possibility of turning the right flank of the Union line. He was distressed to learn there was no way the flanking movement could be successfully achieved. Apparently Jackson attended Lee's council of war held in the Grove house on the square in Sharpsburg after dark. The night was spent at the Smith farm. Jackson slept on the ground.

Thursday, September 18, 1862. One again, Jackson had Hotchkiss search for a crossing of the Potomac in an effort to flank the Union positions. Realizing that Lee would probably order a withdrawal, Jackson had the wounded and all non-essential supplies taken across the Potomac to Shepherdstown. After dark he joined the rest of the command in crossing the Potomac. The first invasion of Maryland was over. But his command had done well, achieving a great victory at Harpers Ferry and A.P. Hill, making a forced march to save Lee's army on the 17th.

Friday, September 19, 1862. Jackson moved toward Martinsburg on the West Virginia side of the river. Some of the men visited Col. A.R. Boteler. The buildings in Shepherdstown were full of Confederate wounded. Lee and his generals took pride in their safe crossing and were thankful to the Almighty for His assistance.

Saturday, September 20, 1862. Fitz John Porter and the Union Fifth Corps crossed the Potomac today and a severe fire fight took place at the ford. Jackson sent A.P. Hill to save the day, which he did. The General wanted good maps of Berkeley County. About dark an order came to go to Tabler's Mill. Jackson had been in the vicinity of Lee Town.

Sunday, September 21, 1862. Jed Hotchkiss found Jackson at Tabler's Mill on the south bank of the Opequon Creek. The stream was full of soldiers bathing themselves and their rags, and trying to get rid of the gray backed lice. The bathing was considered next to godliness.

Monday, September 22, 1862. On the banks of the Opequon Creek.

Tuesday, September 23, 1862. On the banks of the Opequon Creek. Stuart's men were at the Bower,[5] the historic Dandridge home.

Wednesday, September 24, 1862. Moving to Martinsburg for a better campsite. Staff officers hoped conditions would be more sanitary. They hoped to eliminate the lice problem.

Thursday, September 25, 1862. Near Martinsburg.

Friday, September 26, 1862. Near Martinsburg.

Saturday, September 27, 1862. At 5:00 a.m., Jackson's men moved out, keeping to their early hour. They marched through Martinsburg and headed for Bunker Hill. Some of them had camped there in the spring and summer of 1861. Camp was made in back of Mr. Boyd's at Edgewood. This was on the west side of the Valley Pike. It was a warm day. The wounded and those with sore feet were returning to the ranks.

Sunday, September 28, 1862. At Bunker Hill. Dr. Stiles preached this morning.

Monday, September 29, 1862. At Bunker Hill. Jackson gave Hotch-

Jackson Day By Day

kiss, his map maker, a testimonial letter. But he said, "You have a fault, you talk too much."

Tuesday, September 30, 1862. At Bunker Hill.

VIII
THE AUTUMN OF 1862

BUNKER HILL AND THE PANHANDLE

October and the first part of November presented Jackson and his men with a rest and a time to regroup. At Bunker Hill he received many visitors, and a great revival broke out which will be told about in another book.

Wednesday, October 1, 1862. Bunker Hill.

Thursday, October 2, 1862. Bunker Hill.

Friday, October 3, 1862. Bunker Hill.

Saturday, October 4, 1862. Bunker Hill.

Sunday, October 5, 1862. Bunker Hill.

Monday, October 6, 1862. Bunker Hill.

Tuesday, October 7, 1862. At Bunker Hill. The bivouac area was called "Camp Baylor," after the fallen brigade commander. Gen. Lee came to visit Jackson and to discuss strategy. Aides heard the two men talking of Pennsylvania and Maryland. It also seems that the two talked about the conflict between Jackson and A.P. Hill.

Wednesday, October 8, 1862. Bunker Hill.

Thursday, October 9, 1862. Bunker Hill.

Friday, October 10, 1862. Bunker Hill.

Saturday, October 11, 1862. Bunker Hill. Jackson, the former professor was promoted to lieutenant general. He had come a long way.

Sunday, October 12, 1862. Jackson was invited to Holy Communion at Rev. Graham's church in Winchester. However, Jackson could not go. Instead he went to services near headquarters at Bunker Hill and heard Rev. Stiles preach from I Timothy 2:5-6. In a letter to his wife he praised the preacher and said, "It's a glorious thing to be a minister of the Gospel of the Prince of Peace. There is no equal position in the world." The day was damp and rainy.

Monday, October 13, 1862. It was still damp and chilly at Bunker Hill. Jackson was twelve miles from their wartime home in Winchester the previous winter. Headquarters was in a tent.

Tuesday, October 14, 1862. Bunker Hill.

Wednesday, October 15, 1862. Bunker Hill.

Thursday, October 16, 1862. Bunker Hill.

Friday, October 17, 1862. Bunker Hill.

Saturday, October 18, 1862. Bunker Hill.

Sunday, October 19, 1862. Bunker Hill.

Monday, October 20, 1862. Bunker Hill.

Tuesday, October 21, 1862. Bunker Hill.

Wednesday, October 22, 1862. Bunker Hill.

Thursday, October 23, 1862. Headquarters at Bunker Hill.

Friday, October 24, 1862. Headquarters at Bunker Hill. Folks in the area concerned about lack of rain.

Saturday, October 25, 1862. Today, Jackson moved headquarters to Charlestown. Part of the objective was to tear up the Winchester and Potomac Railroad.

Sunday, October 26, 1862. A severe rainstorm hit the area. Confederates in the Charlestown area, and Union soldiers on Maryland Heights suffered from the wind and rain, many losing their tents to the high winds.

Monday, October 27, 1862. Jackson was still at Charlestown.

Tuesday, October 28, 1862. Headquarters moved to Pendleton's near Blackburn's in Clarke County on the Summit Point and Berryville Road, about 4½ miles from Berryville.

According to a Mrs. Lee, today Jackson and his staff came to her house. We wonder if this may have been the day the famous Winchester portrait may have been taken. Jackson may have stopped to Mrs. Lee's, the McGuire's and then the photographer, as he traveled to his new headquarters.

Wednesday, October 29, 1862. At Pendleton's.

Thursday, October 30, 1862. At Pendleton's.

Friday, October 31, 1862. Headquarters was four miles beyond Berryville. This was at Pendleton's or Blackburn's on the Summit Point Road.

Saturday, November 1, 1862. Jackson and Hotchkiss talked about Jed's commission, and about the continued service of the map maker. Headquarters still at Blackburn's.

Sunday, November 2, 1862. A nice autumn day in the West Virginia panhandle. Still near Berryville.

Monday, November 3, 1862. It was cold today. Headquarters was moved to Carter Hall at Millwood, a large estate.

Tuesday, November 4, 1862. Carter Hall.

Wednesday, November 5, 1862. Carter Hall.

Thursday, November 6, 1862. Frank Paxton of Lexington selected as the new commander of the Stonewall Brigade. Headquarters was moved to Saratoga, the Morgan home on the Front Royal and Winchester Road. An early winter storm developed.

Friday, November 7, 1862. Saratoga. Sleet, rain and snow today.

Saturday, November 8, 1862. Saratoga.

Sunday, November 9, 1862. Saratoga. 700 blankets distributed to troops in Winchester.

Monday, November 10, 1862. Saratoga. Jackson receives a telegram from Col. Boteler in Richmond saying that blankets will be sent to the command.

Tuesday, November 11, 1862. Saratoga.

Wednesday, November 12, 1862. Saratoga.

Thursday, November 13, 1862. Saratoga.

Friday, November 14, 1862. Headquarters at Hogg Runn, two and a half miles from Winchester.

Saturday, November 15, 1862. Jackson and Hotchkiss discussed Jed's visit with General Lee near Culpeper Court House.

Sunday, November 16, 1862. Near Winchester. Jackson and most of the staff went to the Kent Street Presbyterian Church and heard Dr. Graham preach. Jackson looked great. Mrs. McDonald was impressed with his bearing. This was to be his last Sunday in Winchester.[1]

Monday, November 17, 1862. At Hogg's Run. Rain and cold. Men in the tents were very uncomfortable.

Tuesday, November 18, 1862. At Hogg's Run.

Wednesday, November 19, 1862. Today Jackson moved to Winchester. He was located just about one hundred yards from Rev. Graham's in a large white house. The dwelling was just back of the manse and Tom could see the home where he and Anna had spent the previous winter. Acording to a letter, Jackson himself had come into Winchester on Monday. He expressed a desire for his wife to be with him and asked her and all Christian people to join him in a prayer for peace.

Thursday, November 20, 1862. In Winchester taking care of administrative detail. In a letter to his wife, describing his quarters in Winchester, he once again shared his faith in Romans 8:28.

Friday, November 21, 1862. Most of the troops moved out of Winchester today. Jackson, however, spent most of the day with Rev. and Mrs. Graham. He must have thought back to the joyous times he had had there the previous winter. Also, he was awaiting the news that he was a father. Lee left Culpeper and was headed toward Fredericksburg. Mrs. Graham felt that Jackson looked very well and was in good spirits. The parsonage family enjoyed his visit, his last with them and in the city of Winchester. The children were permitted to stay up to see the General.[2]

Saturday, November 22, 1862. The General followed his troops today, heading south on the Valley Pike, riding past the Kernstown battlefield, and on to Tumbling Run beyond Strasburg. He stayed the night at Old Stone House. It was a cold day.

Sunday, November 23, 1862. Jackson continued south today to a point near Mount Jackson. He stayed at a house just beyond Mill Creek.

Monday, November 24, 1862. It was back in the saddle for Jackson, riding to New market across the Massanutten Mountains and the Shenandoah via Columbia Bridge. Then it was on to Hawksbill on the road to Madison Court House. Jackson wore the new hat Hotchkiss had bought for him. Some were amazed at his appearance, a new hat and the new uniform coat given him by General Stuart. Jackson blushed and said, "Young Gentlemen, this is no longer the headquarters of the Army of the Valley, but of the Second Corps of the Army of Northern Virginia." The staff, even though in the dark as to his movements, felt this meant that once again they were on their way to join Robert E. Lee.

Tuesday, November 25, 1862. Jackson continued through Fisher's Gap to Madison Court House. Camp was made half a mile beyond the town on the Gordonsville Road. Ewell's Division was nearby.

Wednesday, November 26, 1862. Headquarters on the Gordonsville Road at Madison Court House.

Thursday, November 27, 1862. Headquarters still at Gordonsville.

Friday, November 28, 1862. Jackson moved today to Haxall's, one mile south of Orange Court House. A long awaited letter arrived. Jackson nervously opened it and read, "My Own Dear Father,....I know that you are rejoiced to hear of my coming, and I hope that God has sent me to radiate your pathway through life. I am a very tiny little thing. I weigh only eight and a half pounds...." Still Jackson didn't know whether he had a son or a daughter. He had to turn the page and read "Your dear little wee daughter."[3] Although, like most men, he had hoped for a son, the General accepted the Divine mandate.

Saturday, November 29, 1862. Jackson with an aide and several couriers mounted up and headed for Lee's headquarters on Mine Run Road near Fredericksburg. It was to be a long day in the saddle, around forty miles.

The route was the Orange Plank Road. The home of Rev. Melzi Chancellor was reached about noon. The group stopped to rest, eat, and feed the horses. This was near the Wilderness Church.

Snow was falling when the party started again. By late afternoon Salem Church was reached. Jackson was appalled at the sight of the refugees from Fredericksburg. It was a dismal scene. Folks were heading west on foot and the road was filled with wagons and carts. Inside Salem Church, women and children tried to keep warm near a stove or huddled in blankets.[4]

They found Lee in his tent on Mine Run Road, conversed, and then sought lodging for the night. Mr. Muscoe Garnett was happy to take them in out of the snow. A blazing fire warmed the cold, wet general. After a delicious supper, Jackson slept in a bed, and the others on a nice, thick rug.

Before he ended the day, Jackson took time to write to his wife. He admonished her not to "spoil the darling little thing...(but) give her many kisses from her father."

He was overwhelmed by the kindness of the people. He received all kinds of gifts and provisions. He was also thankful to God for improving his eyes enough so he could write at night. "He continually showers blessings upon me, and that you should have been spared, and our darling little daughter given us fills my heart with overflowing gratitude....My desire is to live entirely and unreservedly to God's glory...."

In terms of a name for the new little girl, he suggested "Julia," after his own mother. He challenged his wife to look upon the new arrival as "a gift from God."

Sunday, November 30, 1862. Jackson and his staff rode down the Telegraph Road. "It was Sunday morning but no church bells were ringing. The streets were almost deserted as were the homes." Barksdale's Mississippi Brigade picketed the front on the Rappahannock River. For a brief time, the men sat in their saddles at the corner of the bank and the churches. Lunch was taken at the home of John Scott.

It snowed during the night and the ground was covered. But warming trend made it all disappear by noon. It turned out to be a pleasant day for Jed Hotchkiss, Jackson's map maker. He turned thirty-four today. Jackson made his headquarters at Mrs. French's home, five miles from Fredericksburg. Lee's headquarters were nearby. Jackson and the staff had tea with Mrs. French, and then at the hour of departure, he took the family Bible, read a lesson and had prayer.

Monday, December 1, 1862. Jackson moved his columns via Telegraph Road to Massaponax Church and then proceeded to the Chandler's at Guiney Station. Here he would spend the next two weeks. This was Fairfield, the home of Thomas Coleman Chandler.[5] It was a large estate and the yard was filled with the tents, flags, and horses of the Second Corps, Army of Northern Virginia.

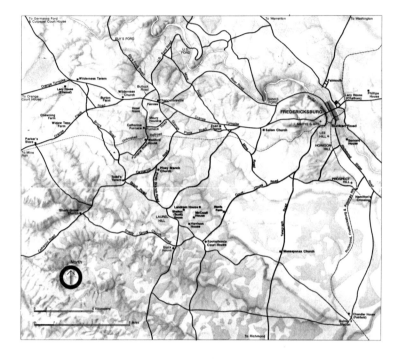

Route to Fredericksburg

IX
FREDERICKSBURG
AND YERBY'S

The rest of Jackson's life was spent in the Fredericksburg area, conducting the battle in mid December, then making winter camp at Moss Neck, and the final camp at Yerby's.

Tuesday, December 2, 1862. Jackson was at headquarters at Chandler's.

Wednesday, December 3, 1862. Headquartered at Chandler's.

Thursday, December 4, 1862. Jackson ordered Jed Hotchkiss to make a map of Caroline County. Jed ate dinner with the commander. Lee also visited the Second Corps Headquarters at Chandler's.

Friday, December 5, 1862. This was a good day to stay in, and Jackson apparently confined himself to planning and administrative tasks. The weather was terrible, a mixture of snow, sleet and rain.

Saturday, December 6, 1862. The roads were in terrible shape from the storm on Friday. Nevertheless, Jackson rode to Lee's headquarters and also into Fredericksburg.

Sunday, December 7, 1862. It rained again today and there were no services. Jackson stayed at headquarters.

Monday, December 8, 1862. Headquarters at Chandeler's.

Tuesday, December 9, 1862. Near Fredericksburg. Jed Hotchkiss was honored with a very precious and unique gift today. Jackson gave him his "Old Gray Hat," worn by the General from December of 1861 until two days before the capture of Harpers Ferry in September of 1862. Jed had bought him a new one in Martinsburg. Like many men, Jackson kept his old one until it was almost worn out. And it wasn't until this December day, almost three months after the purchase, that he asked for it.

Wednesday, December 10, 1862. Near Fredericksburg.

Thursday, December 11, 1862. The Yankees opened with cannon fire on Fredericksburg today and attempted to throw pontoons across the Rappahannock River. Several homes were set on fire, and the city suffered severely. General Barksdale defended against the crossing.

Friday, December 12, 1862. Jackson gave orders for all the staff to be up by 4:00 a.m. and ready to eat. Breakfast finished, Jackson started toward Fredericksburg by the Telegraph Road. On the top of a big hill cannons were placed. Lee was there. But Jackson went to Deep Run to check on the troops. Later, he and Lee rode along the line. Then Jackson rode to Hamilton's Crossing and examined the river bank. He was whistling. Headquarters was made at John Ewing's about two miles from Hamilton's Crossing. A chaplain saw a soldier in an overcoat in the rear of a battery reading a Bible. It was Jackson.

Saturday, December 13, 1862. On the field at Fredericksburg directing the action. Early this morning Jackson rode to Lee's observation point near the top of a hill on Telegraph Road, since known as Lee's Hill. Lee and Jackson looked over the town and expressed confidence they could stop the Yankees.

As Jackson rode back along his lines, cheers rolled like waves "up and down the ranks." Jackson had on a new coat, the gift from his friend Jeb Stuart. He also wore a new sword. His presence was taken as a good omen.

When the fog lifted, the Confederates saw "a grand martial display" ranging far and wide in front of their eyes. The Yankees were coming. "The fluttering flags, the long lines of glittering bayonets, the well dressed officers, the prancing horses, the roll of drums, the notes of bugles..., it was more like a holiday parade...." However, it was no parade. Burnside was ready to make assault after assault on Jackson's lines at Hamilton's Crossing and those of Pete Longstreet on Marye's Heights. Once again, Jackson stood like a "Stonewall" and with his infantry and the guns of Pelham's Horse Artillery beat back the attacks of the enemy. The General watched the action and directed his men from a house near Hamilton's Crossing.[1]

When night fell on the fields covered with the dead and wounded in blue, Jackson and his staff were on a hill near Hamilton's Crossing. He directed James P. Smith to go to Yerby's "and present his regards and sympathy to Maxcy Gregg who was there seriously wounded." Smith found Gregg on "a bed in the center of a large room surrounded by surgeons and other officers.[2] I conveyed my message to him personally. He was much affected and desired me to thank General Jackson for his thoughtful remembrance."

According to Smith, Alexander Boteler and Mr. Volke, the sculptor arrived during the evening. Boteler brought oysters and the cook prepared them. After the hearty meal, Volke asked permission to make some sketches of the General. Still later, Jackson fell asleep on his camp stool while the others were talking.

After dark, there was a tremendous display of the Northern Lights. Jackson inquired of Hunter McGuire the condition of Maxcy Gregg. The doctor left to check on the mortally wounded general. Soon footsteps were heard. Jackson came and spent time alone with Gregg and then rode back to headquarters with Dr. McGuire in silence.

Sunday, December 14, 1862. Never wanting to miss an opportunity to launch a flank attack or inflict loss on the enemy, Jackson was up and at the front at 5:00 a.m.

Monday, December 15, 1862. Today, headquarters of the Second Corps were moved to John Yerby's on the Massaponax. Jackson was off to the front at 5:00 a.m. expecting more action. But it did not come. At 3:00 p.m. the Union General Franklin sent a flag asking for a truce and the opportunity to remove their dead and wounded. At first Jackson refused but yielded upon the receipt of a letter from Franklin.

Tuesday, December 16, 1862. Jackson wrote to his wife saying he was at the front from before dawn until after sunset. "The enemy through God's blessing was repulsed at all points on Saturday and I trust that our Heavenly Father will continue to bless us. We have renewed reason for gratitude to Him for my preservation during the last engagement. We have to mourn the deaths of Generals Maxcy Gregg and Thomas R.R. Cobb. The enemy has recrossed to the north side of the Rappahannock."

When night fell the General and his staff started to prepare camp in the woods. Someone made a fire in a hollow tree and a little later the tree came crashing down.

It was bitter cold that night. Jackson wrapped up in his overcoat and one saddle blanket and covered up with the other. After awhile he sat up and said he was hungry. Apparently Captain Hugh McGuire had taught in the area prior to the war and knew of Moss Neck. So he rode to the Manor and obtained some biscuits and cold ham.

The staff ate. Then Jackson tried his hard cold bed again. Thirty minutes was enough. He stood up and said, "Captain, let's go to the Moss Neck house."

It was midnight when the horsemen of headquarter's Second Corps arrived. Captain McGuire awakened the Corbins. Lights came on. The door was opened and fires started. Jackson was taken to a chamber while James Smith slept on a plush rug, "as comfortable a boy as there was in the army that bitter night. So began our winter's stay at 'Moss Neck.' "[3]

And according to Smith, Jackson had Hugh McGuire, the doctor's brother, to thank.

Moss Neck consisted of large acreage. The mansion had been built by James Park Corbin. The house was on a hill a mile or so back from the Rappahannock River. The home was built on the style of a large English country residence, "with extended wings and large porches." Mrs. Richard Corbin was now running the place. He husband Richard was away at war with the Ninth Virginia Cavalry. Also present at Moss Neck was a sister-in-law Catherine (Kate) Corbin. Soon all the staff officers would be wooing her. However, Sandie Pendelton eventually won.[4]

Wednesday, December 17, 1862. Moss Neck. When morning came, the Corbins gave the General and his staff a hearty breakfast. Mrs. Corbin invited Jackson to stay and use the house as headquarters. He could have as many rooms as he wished. However, the answer as "No." Jackson was grateful. The troops were in the field in the cold and he must share their plight.

The wagons arrived and tents were pitched in a grove beyond the stables. Each man became busy doing his job. Reports came in from the division commanders. Orders were sent to those on picket duty. Messages were sent to Lee and couriers brought messages from the Commanding General and others. Moss Neck became a busy place.

Thursday, December 18, 1862. At Moss Neck. The Confederate line was strengthened by different elements being placed on a line from Port Royal Academy to Rappahannock Academy.

Friday, December 19, 1862. At Moss Neck.

Saturday, December 20, 1862. At Moss Neck. A cold windy day.

Jackson and Jed Hotchkiss looked at maps of Caroline County.

Sunday, December 21, 1862. At Moss Neck. The command rested from their labors of marching from Winchester and the recent battle of Fredericksburg. Many of the staff men, being college men, borrowed books from the excellent selection in the Corbin Library. This evening Jed and Jackson had a long talk. The General said, "War is the greatest of evils." He lamented the troubles the battle had brought upon Fredericksburg. Jackson asked if he throught the troops could endure the cold of winter. Many were without tents and the General thought the weather would be warmer. This must have been a rare moment when Jackson relaxed and talked. He shared his thoughts on railroad accidents and how terrible they were. And he discussed the state of religion in the North and South. The General felt Providence had blessed them so far.

Monday, December 22, 1862. At Moss Neck. Some of the troops began entrenching.

Tuesday, December 23, 1862. At Moss Neck. This was a big day for two of Jackson's staff members. Christmas came early. Sandie Pendleton was promoted to Major and named Assistant Adjutant General, and Hotchkiss was permitted to go home taking care of some army engineering matters on the way. Jackson asked James Smith to prepare a Christmas dinner for Generals Lee, Stuart and Pendleton.[5]

Wednesday, December 24, 1862. At Moss Neck. Pickets on either side of the Rappahannock sang carols to each other. Jackson received a lock of his daughter's hair.

Thursday, December 25, 1862. In 1860 the nation was troubled and on the verge of war, and Jackson spent his last Christmas in Lexington. Christmas of 1861 was spent in Winchester with his wife. That was Jackson's last Christmas with his family. And Christmas 1862 was his last Christmas on earth. He had a few brief months to live. It was a lovely warm day on the banks of the Rappahannock River.

A delicious Christmas dinner was held in the decorated office. James P. Smith apparently supervised it all. Lee and Stuart were there. The menu consisted of turkey, oysters and other goodies. Rev. Pendleton offered the prayer of thanksgiving.

Jackson wrote home saying how much he desired to see his daughter, "and I earnestly pray for peace. Oh that our country was such a Christian, God-fearing people as it should be!"

After the Generals left, the younger officers were entertained at a party in one of the large Corbin parlors.

As Henry Kyd Douglas left he had some thoughts of spending Christmas with those "I laughed with one year ago and of many who laughed with me, who will laugh no more in this world. May this be the last year of this war, I would earnestly pray." Sandie Pendleton wrote, "No chimes of gladness at the recurring anniversary of the advent of the Prince of Peace....We in camp watching the Yankees, and only anxious as to the duration of the war."[6]

Friday, December 26, 1862. At Moss Neck.

Saturday, December 27, 1862. At Moss Neck.

Sunday, December 28, 1862. At Moss Neck. Jackson attended church near General Hill's headquarters. He enjoyed the services very much.

Monday, December 29, 1862. At Moss Neck. Henry Kyd Douglas of Shepherdstown was officially named Inspector General of the Stonewall Brigade. Col. Charles James Faulkner, late Minister to France, came to Jackson's headquarters.

Tuesday, December 30, 1862. At Moss Neck.

Wednesday, December 31, 1862. At Moss Neck, as the final day of 1862 dawned and the last moments ticked away. It had been quite a year for Thomas Jonathan Jackson. Two years ago he was just a lightly regarded professor at VMI. Now he was a national figure, considered a military genius.

He had started the year with an ill-fated expedition to Romney. And then caused great alarm in the North and relieved Confederate armies in eastern Virginia by his brilliant Shenandoah Valley Campaign. He was not at his best during the Seven Days, but led another brilliant flank movement at Second Manassas and stood firm at Antietam and Fredericksburg.

Among his other duties, Jackson took time to write to Colonel Boteler saying,[7] "I have repeatedly urged upon General Lee the importance of protecting the Valley....I am well satisfied that General Lee desires to protect the Valley...."

"It is but natural that I should feel a deep and abiding in-

John W. Schildt   93

terest in the people of the Valley, where are the homes of so many of my brave soldiers who have been with me so long and whose self-sacrificing patriotism has been so thoroughly tested. Apart from this the tried loyalty of those who are still there and their many acts of kindness to me personally,...give me a special interest in that section of the State."

X
WINTER 1863

This month spent at Moss Neck was one for the General and his staff to catch up on administrative detail. Jackson was a stickler for this. We have seen how he was in terms of time and obeying orders to the letter.

But Romney, the Valley, Seven Days, Second Manassas, the Maryland Campaign, and Fredericksburg had given him no time to think about and compose reports. This was now the duty of the hour. And the bulk of the work fell to Sandie Pendleton.

Moss Neck was a good place to work. James Boswell writes, "This is one of the most highly improved estates on the Rappahannock."[1]

Thursday, January 1, 1863. Moss Neck.

Friday, January 2, 1863. At Moss Neck. Jackson rode with Boswell, Robert Rodes and A.P.H. Hill inspecting D.H. Hill's lines. Jackson was not pleased, and recommended the line proposed by Boswell.

Saturday, January 3, 1863. This evening, Jed Hotchkiss took Jackson some apples and chestnuts and read him the news confirming the Confederate victory at Murfreesboro. This made the entire staff very happy. Jackson contributed $100 to a fund aimed to help the homeless and suffering in Fredericksburg.

Sunday, January 4, 1863. Today was warm with a light sprinkle. Jackson went to Grace Church for worship services. The church was full. Mrs. Robert Rodes was in attendance. Seeing her made the General wish for the presence of Mrs. Jackson. Rev. Friend preached.

Monday, January 5, 1863. Jackson spent most of the day at his Moss Neck headquarters.

Tuesday, January 6, 1863. Today there was a review of A.P. Hill's Division at the Hayfield estate. It was a lovely military sight, marred only by a slow, cold drizzle. Hotchkiss and Jackson discussed troop conditions in the evening. Boswell felt Hill's division was the finest in the Confederate army, and Hill had no superior.

Jackson wrote home saying he was glad his wife and daughter were better. "I trust that we all three may so live as to most glorify His holy name...." The General was glad to be quartered inside, his ears were bothering him and he felt he could no longer endure the same rigors as the summer of 1862. Some cases of smallpox had developed in the camps and he advised his wife to wait until spring to come for a visit.[2]

Thursday, January 8, 1863. At Moss Neck. Jackson entertained Jeb Stuart, von Borcke and Henry Douglas for dinner. Colonel Faulkner[3] had been appointed to prepare reports.

Friday, January 9, 1863. At Moss Neck.

Saturday, January 10, 1863. At Moss Neck. It rained today and some of the staff officers availed themselves of the Corbin's fine library. James Boswell spent most of the day in his tent reading "The Tale of Two Cities."

Sunday, January 11, 1863. At Moss Neck.

Monday, January 12, 1863. At Moss Neck.

Tuesday, January 13, 1863. At Moss Neck.

Wednesday, January 14, 1863. At Moss Neck.

Thursday, January 15, 1863. At Moss Neck.

Friday, January 16, 1863. At Moss Neck. Jackson received a letter from his wife four days after it was written. He lamented the slow conveyance of the mails and felt the Confederate mails were not much better than the U.S. mail. The fact the letter did not travel on Sunday made him happy. What a difference today.

Saturday, January 17, 1863. At Moss Neck. Jackson replied to his wife's letter talking about the delights of their heavenly home. He also said, "I am gratified at hearing that you have commenced disciplining the baby. Now be careful and don't let her conquer you....How I would love to see the little darling; whom I love so tenderly, though I have never seen her; and if the war were only over,...I would hurry down to North Carolina to see my wife and baby....Can't you send her to me by express?"[4]

Col. Faulkner was a great help in making reports, and Captain William Allan of Winchester is the new chief of ordnance. Jackson was sorry "to see our Winchester friends again in the hands of the enemy." The General received several presents today, a pair of gauntlets "from near the Potomac, and another beautiful pair from Mrs. Preston Trotter."

Sunday, January 18, 1863. At Moss Neck.

Monday, January 19, 1863.

Tuesday, January 20, 1863. At Moss Neck. Jeb Stuart had a big cavalry review today near "Moss Neck mansions" for the benefit of Generals Lee and Jackson.

Wednesday, January 21, 1863. At Moss Neck. Jackson's last birthday.

Thursday, January 22, 1863. At Moss Neck.

Friday, January 23, 1863. Moss Neck. Eighteen inches of snow fell in the Shenandoah Valley. However, along the Rappahannock near Moss Neck, it was foggy and misty. Jackson and Hotchkiss checked a map of the position of the Second Corps and discussed defensive points.

Saturday, January 24, 1863. In camp at Moss Neck. In the evening Jackson scans a copy of the "New York Herald." It states that New York must speak for peace, and that Jackson is a slavery fanatic.

Sunday, January 25, 1863. Moss Neck.

Monday, January 26, 1863. Moss Neck.

Tuesday, January 27, 1863. Moss Neck.

Wednesday, January 28, 1863. Moss Neck. Wet snow most of the day. Very disagreeable weather. Jackson was pleased with a completed map of the Moss Neck line. Today Jackson finished his report on the Battle of Fredericksburg.

Thursday, January 29, 1863. Moss Neck. Encampment covered with a foot of snow.

Friday, January 30, 1863. Moss Neck.

Saturday, January 31, 1863. At Moss Neck. Captain Bushy of the British Army called upon Jackson today and gave him a waterproof oil cloth "in which to sleep on a wet night in summer campaigning."

———————— February 1863 ————————

Quartered throughout the month at Moss Neck.

Sunday, February 1, 1863. At Moss Neck. Roads were in bad shape. The General and staff confined largely to quarters. The Stonewall Brigade finished their new log chapel.

Monday, February 2, 1863. A nice winter day.

Tuesday, February 3, 1863. At Moss Neck. Jackson wrote home this winter day.
"In answer to the prayers of God's people, I trust He will soon give us peace. I haven't seen my wife for nearly a year — my home in nearly two years, and have never seen our darling little daughter; but it is important that I, and those at headquarters, should set an example of remaining at the post of duty....My old Stonewall Brigade has built a log church. As yet I have not been in it. I am much interested in reading Hunter's LIFE OF MOSES. It is a delightful book."[5]
It was cold today. Jackson was visited by Hotchkiss who was seeking a leave of absence.

Wednesday, February 4, 1863. At Moss Neck. A cold winter day.

Thursday, February 5, 1863. At Moss Neck. Snow and rain.

Friday, February 6, 1863. At Moss Neck. Col. M.G. Harman and William J. Bell of Staunton gave Jackson an excellent horse today.

Saturday, February 7, 1863. At Moss Neck. "This has been a beautiful spring day. I have been thinking lately about gardening. If I were at home, it would be time for me to begin to prepare the hot-bed."

Sunday, February 8, 1863. At Moss Neck. Jackson and Henry Douglas rode to the Stonewall Brigade Chapel. Services were in progress when they arrived. Jackson asked Henry to see if it was full. It was. The General did not wish to disturb the service by a late entrance. He went elsewhere but returned for the 3:00 p.m. service.

Monday, February 9, 1863. At Moss Neck.

Tuesday, February 10, 1863. At Moss Neck.

Wednesday, February 11, 1863. At Moss Neck.

Thursday, February 12, 1863. At Moss Neck.

Friday, February 13, 1863. At Moss Neck.

Saturday, February 14, 1863. At Moss Neck.

Sunday, February 15, 1863. At Moss Neck.

Monday, February 16, 1863. At Moss Neck.

Tuesday, February 17, 1863. At Moss Neck.

Wednesday, February 18, 1863. At Moss Neck.

Thursday, February 19, 1863. At Moss Neck. Mud covered the area. Jackson and Faulkner were quite busy on reports. Jed Hotchkiss returned from furlough and had a long talk with the commander.

Friday, February 20, 1863. At Moss Neck. Faulkner worked on a report of the Battle of McDowell. Jed did a map of Winchester. Jackson took steps to cut down desertion. Three members of the Stonewal Brigade were whipped.

Saturday, February 21, 1863. At Moss Neck. Jackson working on Court Martial proceedings, taking place at Moss Neck.

Sunday, February 22, 1863. At Moss Neck. The Yankees fired salutes in honor of George Washington's birthday. Jackson and Hotchkiss discussed Dr. Hoge's[6] mission to Europe in an effort to procure Bibles. A big snow storm hit Moss Neck.

Monday, February 23, 1863. At Moss Neck in deep snow. Jackson ordered Hotchkiss to secretly prepare a "map of the Valley of Va." extended to Harrisburg, Pa.

Tuesday, February 24, 1863. At Moss Neck.

Wednesday, February 25, 1863. Headquarters at Moss Neck. Today James Boswell observed his first anniversary as a member of Jackson's staff. Perhaps his thouhts were like those of the General.

"How long it seems since that day; it appears more like ten years than one; the truth is that I have thought, felt and acted more in the last year than in all the rest of my life. During the year I have been present in ten hard-fought and bloody battles, besides a number of skirmishes. I have been once with General Jackson when he was defeated, and nine times when he was victorious; in some of these battles I have been exposed to death in all its forms, and in others I have been exposed but little. I have heard the wild cry of victory as it rose above the roar of the cannon and musket. I have seen the field strewn with thousands of corpses, both of friend and foe. I have heard the groans of the wounded and dying. I have seen the fairest portions of the Old Dominion desolated by the ravages of...war. I have seen towns ransacked, and hundred, nay thousands, of helpless women and children thrown homeless upon the world. I have seen our noble leader, General Lee, again and again on the field of battle....O war, why art thou called glorious when such are thy fruits? How long must our dear land be desolated by the ravages and our bravest sacrificed upon thy altars?....One year ago I was full of life and animation, hope dressed the future in 'coleur de rose,' all my dreams were cherished as though I were sure of their realization."[7]

Boswell had less than three months to live when he wrote this. He had a rendezvous with death at Chancellorsville.

Thursday, February 26, 1863. Moss Neck.

Friday, February 27, 1863. Moss Neck.

Saturday, February 28, 1863. Moss Neck. Jackson received a box of presents today from a lady in England. A deserter was shot.

————— March 1863 —————

The first part of the month was spent at Moss Neck. Then the command moved after three months to Yerby's.

Sunday, March 1, 1863. Moss Neck. Almost like spring. Jed Hotchkiss dined at Jackson's tent today, and later rode down to the river with Dr. Hunter McGuire. Rev. Mr. Lacy came to headquarters today.

Monday, March 2, 1863. Moss Neck. A pleasant day.

Tuesday, March 3, 1863. Moss Neck.

Wednesday, March 4, 1863. Moss Neck.

Thursday, March 5, 1863. Moss Neck. Jed, Pendleton and Jackson had quite a time over the conscription question. Lee had ordered all men enrolled and listed in company rosters. It was a matter or red tape and paperwork, but very upsetting.

Friday, March 6, 1863. Moss Neck.

Saturday, March 7, 1863. Moss Neck.

Sunday, March 8, 1863. Moss Neck. Dr. Hoge gave a very powerful sermon at the Stonewall Brigade Chapel, preaching on the death of Stephen. The men knew about death, they lost 1,890 men in 1862. And Dr. McGuire buried his servant today.

Monday, March 9, 1863. Moss Neck.

Tuesday, March 10, 1863. Moss Neck. Snow flurries. Hotchkiss worked on maps of Kernstown.

Wednesday, March 11, 1863. Moss Neck. Jackson and Sandie Pendleton worked on reports for the Battle of Winchester.

Thursday, March 12, 1863. Moss Neck. Jackson went to Lee's tent this morning. Jackson was very much pleased with the maps leading to the action at Winchester. Lee left for Richmond this afternoon.

Friday, March 13, 1863. Moss Neck. Jackson signed Boswell's letter recommending Jed Hotchkiss for a commission in the Prov.

Engineering Corps and assignment to the Second Corps.

Saturday, March 14, 1863. Moss Neck.

Sunday, March 15, 1863. Moss Neck. Jackson went to church today sharing services with his old command, "The Stonewall
Brigade." He wore a plain cap without the gold lace. The sermon was "Occupy till I Come." The afternoon was stormy;
sleet, hail, then thunder and lightning.

Monday, March 16, 1863. This was Jackson's last full day at Moss
Neck. The engineers and quartermaster detachments moved
"at an early hour" to the home of Thomas Yerby, about two
miles from Hamilton's Crossing. Jackson visited the ailing little
Janie Corbin. He gave her his gold braid.

Tuesday, March 17, 1863. Today Jackson left Moss Neck. It must
have been a sad time. He had been there for three months con-
tinuously. Jed Hotchkiss says "we...have had quite a pleasant
winter, all things considered." Boswell spoke for all when he
said, "I fear that our memories of this camp will be by no
means as pleasant as those of Moss Neck, for we have certainly been most fortunate in our winter quarters, and we shall
always look back to the three months spent at Moss Neck with
no small degree of pleasure. Mrs. Corbin and Miss Kate shall
always have my best wishes."[8]
    Sandie Pendleton and Hunter McGuire came and took soup
with the rest of the command.
    The sound of heavy cannonading was heard. This was an
omen of things to come. And there was a severe cavalry skirmish at Kelley's Ford. In this action, Major John Pelham,[9] the
commander of the Horse Artillery fell mortally wounded.
    Belvoir, sometimes spelled Bellvoir, was the main home of
Thomas Yerby, "south of Hamilton's Crossing and below
Massaponax Creek," was built in the late 1700's. In 1827 the
Pratt's of Smithfield bought it from the Herndon's and
transferred it to their kinfolk, the Yerby's. This is a prominent
name in the Fredericksburg area.
    Thomas Yerby, not William, as many think, owned Belvoir
and lived there during the Civil War. Here McGuire treated
Gregg, and Jackson came to see the dying lieutenant. And
Robert E. Lee recovered from a serious illness here in the
spring of 1863.[10]
    Sadly, the house burned to the ground in 1906. However,
the family burying ground is still intact.

Wednesday, March 18, 1863. Yerby's. Janie Corbin, the darling of Moss Neck dies. Jackson weeps.

Thursday, March 19, 1863. Yerby's. Jackson, Pendleton and McGuire had a big discussion about forage.

Friday, March 20, 1863. At Yerby's. Bad weather set in. It stormed all night.

Saturday, March 21, 1863. At Yerby's. More bad weather; snow and sleet.

Sunday, March 22, 1863. At Yerby's. Naturally there was church. Rev. Lacy spoke on "The blood of Abel and the blood of Christ." Jackson listened very closely.

Monday, March 23, 1863. At Yerby's, Pendleton working on battle reports, and Jed Hotchkiss on maps. One of his friends came by and said that Jackson's sister was a Yankee woman. "She could take care of the wounded Feds as fast as brother Thomas could wound them." The snow was two feet deep in the Shenandoah.

Tuesday, March 24, 1863. At Yerby's. Mild and pleasant until afternoon when it started to rain. Lee came to see Jackson.
　　Hotchkiss visited Jeb Stuart and discussed the battle at Kelly's Ford. He said his cavalry never performed better. Like everyone else, he lamented the loss of "the gallant Pelham."
　　This evening, James Boswell brought Jackson a can of fresh peaches from his grandmother. The General expressed great delight. He loved his fruit.

Wednesday, March 25, 1863. Yerby's.

Thursday, March 26, 1863. Yeby's. Col. Faulkner told Hotchkiss how Jackson told him that during the next battle he was to observe the action and write it down immediately so there would not be so many conflicting statements.

Friday, March 27, 1863. Yerby's. This was a day set aside for prayer and fasting. Naturally, Jackson and the Second Corps observed the day. Jackson led in prayer at 8:00 a.m.
　　The day was like Sunday with over fifty services conducted by chaplains and others. Dr. Lacy spoke at Yerby's from Matthew 21:44 stressing national responsibility to God. At 5:00 p.m. there was a prayer meeting. Jackson and others hoped

that much good might come from the Lord as a result of their prayers.

Saturday, March 28, 1863. Yerby's.

Sunday, March 29, 1863. Yerby's. Services were held at headquarters today. The theme was trust God, but do your best and pray. The congregation was deeply touched by the power of the message. Jed Hotchkiss read the Lesson. At 6:00 p.m. some of the staff gathered in Lacy's tent for a prayer meeting. "The General prayed fervently for peace and for blessings on our enemies in everything but the war." In the evening, Jackson went to see Lee who was sick.

Monday, March 30, 1863. Yerby's.

Tuesday, March 31, 1863. Yerby's.

—————— April 1863 ——————

Jackson's final full month of life was spent at Yerby's. The highlight of the month was the arrival of Mrs. Jackson and little Julia on April 20, Julia's baptism on the 23rd, and General and Mrs. Jackson going to church together on the 26th. Jackson also posed for his last picture at Yerby's.

Wednesday, April 1, 1863. Yerby's. March had gone out like a lion with snow and sleet. But today the snow melted. A large group gathered at Rev. Lacy's tent for a 6:00 p.m. prayer meeting.

Thursday, April 2, 1863. Yerby's.

Friday, April 3, 1863. Yerby's. Jackson was upset today over some of the map work done on the Cedar Mountain campaign.

Saturday, April 4, 1863. Yerby's. Jackson and Faulkner had quite a discussion on simplicity and brevity in military reports. Although Jackson would take an officer to task, he wanted nothing in a report that reflected on a man's ability. Faulkner and Jackson discussed the strategy involved at Port Republic. It snowed again tonight.

Sunday, April 5, 1863. Yerby's. The snow was six inches deep this morning, most unusual. Services were held at Mr. Lacy's tent. The text was from Romans 8:28, "All things work together for good for those who love the Lord." This was Jackson's favorite verse.

Monday, April 6, 1863. Yerby's. Jackson and Hotchkiss went over the Cedar Run maps. The map maker felt he had never seen a more exact or precise man. Everything had to be correct.

Tuesday, April 7, 1863. Yerby's. Jackson's friend Jeb Stuart spent most of the day with him.

Wednesday, April 8, 1863. Yerby's. Yesterday Stuart came to visit Jackson. Today it was Lee's turn. The commander came in the afternoon.

Thursday, April 9, 1863. Yerby's. Apparently to be a quite routine day.

Friday, April 10, 1863. Yerby's. Routine day. After dinner Hotchkiss rode into Fredericksburg, "looking at the many evidences of the hard fought field that were visible; torn trees, battered walls, broken houses....The evidence of grim visaged war hang as clouds amid the brightness."

Saturday, April 11, 1863. Yerby's. Jed brought Jackson the map of Port Republic today. Jackson had but one change to make, "Instead of 'Valley Army' at one place on it, I should put 'Army of the Valley.' " This shows how precise Jackson was.[11]

Sunday, April 12, 1863. Yerby's. Mr. Lacy preached a fine sermon with a large crowd. Late in the afternoon it rained.

Monday, April 13, 1863. Yerby's. A routine day.

Tuesday, April 14, 1863. Yerby's. Jackson and Hotchkiss spent a lot of time in discussing a variety of subjects. Jackson said he liked teaching and was fond of Spanish. Then he switched to the scenery at New River, and his only sister, and those of his family who had died. He received a nice scarf from a Maryland lady living in La. General Lee came again.

Wednesday, April 15, 1863. Yerby's. Jackson was somewhat confused on about his dates and movements from Port Republic to

Richmond. He compared the Union engineers with the Confederates and felt the Union men were better. Jackson finally approved the reports of Port Republic and sent them in. Boswell returned from Richmond and shared the news that pencils were now a dollar each.

Thursday, April 16, 1863. Yerby's.

Friday, April 17, 1863. Yerby's. The Yankees sent gunboats up the Rappahannock River today causing a great commotion. Jackson had couriers going all over the place, and ordered the artillery to be ready to move at a moment's notice. The Yankees had balloons up in the air to observe the Confederate lines. Col. Faulkner finished his reports "of all of Gen. J's battles."

Saturday, April 18, 1863. Yerby's. Jackson would have loved the health food fads of today. He followed a different diet. And in discussing rations, told Jed that rice was more nutritious than beans, and then gave facts to prove his point.

Sunday, April 19, 1863. Yerby's. Rev. Lacy preached today.

Monday, April 20, 1863. Yerby's. It was raining today, but that did not matter. A train was due to arrive at Guiney Station. And Jackson went to meet it. On board were his wife and daughter. This was to be their initial meeting, father and daughter. Mrs. Jackson describes the encounter.

"When he entered the coach to receive us his rubber raincoat was dripping from the rain,...but his face was all sunshine and gladness...."[11]

The General looked lovingly at his daughter, but because of his wet coat would not take her in his arms.

"The soldiers cheered them loudly when they saw him and her together."[12]

When they reached Yerby's, the family went to the room occupied by General Lee in his illness. Jackson threw off his wet coat, took the little girl in his arms and held her for a long time, making all the noises of a new father. He studied her face, and later when she fell asleep, knelt by the cradle to study her features.

Tuesday, April 21, 1863. With the family at Yerby's. They had given the Jackson's "a large, comfortable room,...which was hospitably furnished."[13]

Jackson Day By Day

Wednesday, April 22, 1863. With the family at Yerby's.

Thursday, April 23, 1863. Today little Julia was five months old. General and Mrs. Jackson decided this was to be the day of her baptism. Reverend Tucker Lacy was selected to perform the rite. It was to be a private service, but young James P. Smith requested special permission to attend. The proud father told him to bring the rest of the staff along.

The appointed hour came and the room of the Yerby home filled with the staff officers of the Second Corps, Army of Northern Virginia. Jackson, always a stickler for punctuality, found that women and children do not move like soldiers. Mrs. Jackson and little Julia were a few minutes late for the service.[14]

Today and during her stay, Mrs. Jackson was visited by a whole host of Confederate officers coming to see her and little Stonewall. Mrs. Jackson did very well in her meetings. However, she held General Lee in awe, and almost panicked when he was around.

Friday, April 24, 1863. At Yerby's, headquarters and with the family. More rain.

Saturday, April 25, 1863. At Yerby's.

Sunday, April 26, 1863. At Yerby's. Jackson had but two weeks left, but no one knew that this fine April Sabbath. Julia's baptism had been one big event with the General, and today brought another one.

Throughout the war, Jackson had gone to church and observed other officers at worship with their wives. Today was his turn. Anna went to church with him. Many of his lieutenants were there with their wives, along with several thousand men of the Second Corps. In light of what was about to happen, a good text would have been, "Do not brag about tomorrow for you do not know what a day will bring forth."[15] Lacy's message was on the rich man and Lazarus.

It was a most memorable sabbath,...

"being the last upon which I was privileged to attend divine services with my husband on earth, and to worship in camp with such a company of soldiers as I had never seen together in a religious congregation. My husband took me in an ambulance to his headquarters where the services were held, and on the way were seen streams of officers and soldiers, some riding, some walking, all wending their way to the place of worship....We found Mr. Lacy in a tent in which we were seated together with General Lee and other distinguished officers. I remember how reverent and impressive was General Lee's bearing, and how handsome he looked with his splendid figure and military attire. In front of the tent,...were spread out in dense masses the soldiers sitting upon benches or standing."[16]

The singing was good, the preaching was excellent. It was a great Sunday morning. Jackson spent all of Sunday afternoon with his wife. He seemed in excellent health and spirits, and discussed spiritual things.

Monday, April 27, 1863. With the family at Yerby's, giving them every possible moment. Time was growing short. Jackson was in his last week. General Lee told Boswell that Hooker was planning to advance but the rain had delayed him. Lee came to see Jackson.

Tuesday, April 28, 1863. With the family at Yerby's.

Wednesday, April 29, 1863. Dawn came to the Fredericksburg area. The Jackson family was asleep at Yerby's. Suddenly the General was aroused by loud knocking. It was an officer from General Early with news of a possible Union advance. Perhaps this was the Union spring offensive. If so, it mean battle, and Anna and the baby might not be safe at Yerby's. They had better go back to Richmond. He must go, he would return if possible to see her off. If not, he would send her brother Joseph Morrison to take care of her. Mrs. Jackson shares their last moments.

"After a tender and hasty good-bye, he hurried off without breakfast. Scarcely had he gone when the roar of cannons began." Soon Rev. Lacy was at the door with an ambulance to take Mrs. Jackson to the train station. The General had sent a note expressing his regrets over not being able to come, and invoking God's blessing on them.[17]

Thursday, April 30, 1863. Jackson spent a long time in devotions on Wednesday night. The General was up long before dawn taking care of the details of striking the camp. The air was damp and mist shrouded the bivouac area. Officers and men noted the intensity of Jackson. He was ready for combat. Just before his own tent was struck, Jackson went in for a last minute moment of prayer. This was the last time he used the tent.

Then he rode off to meet with Lee. When they met, apparently near Lee's Hill, the two commanders in gray observed the Union lines. Jackson wanted to make an attack. However, Lee gently reminded him that the situation was much like that of December 13 when the Confederates were unable to follow the Yankees due to their gun emplacements on Stafford Heights. Lee permitted Jackson to do some more scouting before making a final decision not to attack.

Then the two decided to leave units to hold Fredericksburg while moving westward to the Wilderness where they would be free to maneuver against the Army of the Potomac. Perhaps they could even trap Hooker near the point where the Rapidan and Rappahannock Rivers met.

XI
THEN COMETH
THE END

April was gone. A new month had come, and with it both the necessity and opportunity for action. The result was a model military move, but then disaster for the Confederacy.

Friday, May 1, 1863. Jackson was up before 1:00 a.m. looking sharp in a full dress uniform. Daylight hours could not be wasted. The troops were roused, and Jackson himself led the troops of Robert Rodes, A.P. Hill and Colston. The Second Corps must reach a point to be able to thwart the advance of the Army of the Potomac. "Down the Plank Road from Fredericksburg to Orange Court House swung the long line of lean veterans."[1]

Sounds of fighting could be heard. The troops of General Anderson were locked in combat with the advance of the Union army. Jackson was anxious to attack Hooker before he could get out of the woods and into open country to deploy his larger army.

Jackson was cheered by his men, and they were ordered to press the Union forces back toward Chancellorsville, west of Fredericksburg. The General observed the action and expressed confidence in a great victory. He gave the countersign for the evening, "Challenge, Liberty; Reply, Independence."[2]

Later in the evening, Jeb Stuart reported that Hooker's right flank was not anchored by a natural barrier or entrenchments. This was a golden opportunity. Now a way to approach the flank without being spotted was needed. The question, "How can we get at those people?"

Saturday, May 2, 1863. About midnight, James Power Smith got awake. Near him two figures were sitting around a little campfire. There at the junction of the Orange Plank Road and the Furnace Road, Robert E. Lee and Thomas J. Jackson were planning their move against Joseph Hooker. Chaplain Lacy, a native of the area was called to give advice on the roads. Charles Wellford would be a good guide.

With the coming of the dawn, the veterans of the Second Corps were tramping through the woods. Union scouts thought they were retreating. By late in the afternoon the command was west of the lines of the Union Eleventh Corps commanded by Oliver O. Howard. Jackson told Robert Rodes, "You may go forward." And with that the great Confederate flank attack was unleashed.

About nine o'clock Jackson rode forward to assess the situation. Confederate troops mistook Jackson and his staff for the enemy and opened fire. Jackson was hit twice in the left arm and once in the right hand. The bone and artery of the left arm were shattered. Jackson lost a lot of blood, and at one point the litter fell. Smith and Morrison protected the General with their own bodies.

At the home of Rev. Melzi Chancellor, Jackson was examined by Dr. McGuire. Then there was a three-mile ride by army ambulance to the field hospital overlooking Wilderness Run.

Sunday, May 3, 1863. After midnight, Dr. McGuire told Jackson they would administer chloroform and probe the wound. The ball in the right hand was taken out without much difficulty. Then about 2:00 a.m. McGuire amputated the left arm. The operation was successful, and by mid-morning, Jackson talked with Sandie Pendleton and others about the battle and about the Sunday services. Jackson dictated a note naming Stuart as his successor and heard a note of sympathy from General Lee.[3]

Then orders came from General Lee to move Jackson to a safer spot. When asked if he had any choice, the General recalled the kindness of the Chandler family at Guiney Station the previous December.

The battle of Chancellorsville, a great Confederate victory, concluded today. However, it was clouded by the wounding of Jackson, and the army hoped and prayed for his rapid recovery.

Monday, May 4, 1863. Early this morning Jackson was placed in an army ambulance for the long ride to Chandler's. Jed Hotchkiss took some engineers to make sure the Brock Road leading to Spotsylvania Court House was clear. Dr. McGuire, Chaplain Lacy and Officer Smith rode with Jackson. Along the route men and women rushed to the ambulance. Some brought food. Many were in tears, and all said they were praying for his recovery.

The General "bore the journey well and was cheerful throughout the day." Beverly Lacy made arrangements with Mrs. Chandler to use the little office building to shelter Jackson. The ambulance arrived about 8:00 p.m. and the General was ready for sleep.[4]

Tuesday, May 5, 1863. Dr. McGuire changed bandages. The wounds looked like they were healing. Jackson had a good breakfast, and Chaplain Lacy led morning devotions. The General requested the clergyman to come every morning. The building was ideal. Smith had a room upstairs, another room was used by the doctors and as a kitchen. And Dr. McGuire had a couch in the room with Jackson. This may have been the day when Jackson discussed the model battlefield reports found in the Scriptures.[5]

Wednesday, May 6, 1863. It was rainy today, but no gloom at Fairfield. Jackson was cheerful and continued his theological discussions with young Smith. He quoted from his favorite verse, "All things work together for good for those who love the Lord." Romans 8:28. The wound in the right hand hurt more than the arm. Mrs. Jackson who was staying with Mrs. Hoge in Richmond received the news of her husband's wounds today.

Thursday, May 7, 1863. Dr. McGuire, exhausted by his constant vigil and attention to Jackson, fell asleep late on Wednesday. Early this morning Jackson became nauseated. He instructed his servant Jim to apply a wet towel. He did not want to awaken Dr. McGuire. However, the pain in his side became worse, and at dawn McGuire checked his patient. He recognized the onset of pneumonia.[6] Things did not look good. Mrs. Jackson, little Julia and Nurse Hetty arrived from Richmond. Mrs. Jackson became unnerved as she saw a body being examined in the yard. It was that of a Lexington friend and neighbor, General Frank Paxton. "This was a chilling introduction to Fairfield." She was also upset by her husband's pain and labored breathing.[7]

Friday, May 8, 1863. Today Jackson seemed to be holding his own. He was not much improved, but he was no worse. He expressed confidence that he would live. Although he was not afraid to die, he believed God still had work for him to do on earth.

Saturday, May 9, 1863. Jackson was weaker today, yet he had moments of insight. He remarked to Dr. McGuire, "I see from the number of physicians that you think my condition dangerous, but I thank God, if it is His will, that I am ready to go."[8]

He asked for Julia and touched her hand and talked to her. Fluid was filling the lungs and talking was difficult. Still he asked Chaplain Lacy about the upcoming church services.

Anna read to him. Naturally it was from the Bible. Then he asked her to sing. For her it was most difficult, but she sang the lines of the fifty-first Psalm, "Shew pity, Lord; O Lord, forgive."

Sunday, May 10, 1863. Early in the morning, Mrs. Jackson informs him that he is gravely ill and that he should be prepared for the worst. He stated that it would be gain to be translated to Heaven. The General shared with his wife the hope that she would return to her home if he did not make it, and requested burial in Lexington. As the morning progressed Jackson grew worse. At 11:00 a.m. his wife kneels beside his bed and tells him that before the day is over he will be with his Saviour. He tries to comfort his wife who breaks down. Sandie Pendleton comes in and the General asks, "Who is preaching at head-quarters today?" Sandie told him the entire army was praying for him. Jackson was grateful and said, "It's the Lord's day; my wish is fulfilled. I have always desired to die on Sunday."[9]

From then on he became delirious at times, talking of the staff, battle, the family and prayer. Then "Order A.P. Hill to prepare for action! Pass the infantry to the front rapid-ly....And a little later let us pass over the river and rest under the shade of the trees."[10] The Great Captain was gone.

Sandie Pendleton rode to the telegraph office and sent a message to Richmond saying "General Jackson died at fifteen minutes past three afternoon."[11]

Monday, May 11, 1863. A train leaves from Guiney Station taking the body of Thomas Jonathan Jackson to Richmond. Members of the staff were on board. People lined the tracks. Then a horse drawn hearse carried the casket covered with the Con-federate flag through the streets of Richmond to the Gover-nor's Mansion. The bells of the city tolled in sadness.

Tuesday, May 12, 1863. At 10:00 a.m. the body of General Jackson was taken to the Capitol of the State of Virginia. Even the musicians playing the funeral dirges wept. There was never a sadder time in Richmond.[12]

Wednesday, May 13, 1863. Funeral services were held in Richmond today. The funeral train left for Lynchburg. On board with the fallen leader was the Jackson family, Sandie Pendleton, James P. Smith and Dr. McGuire.

Thursday, May 14, 1863. The train reached Lynchburg and the

body was transferred to a boat called "The Marshall." A detachment of VMI cadets met the body and escorted it back to the campus where Jackson had taught. In fact, the casket was placed in one of his old lecture halls.

Friday, May 15, 1863. This morning Jackson's funeral procession moved from the campus of VMI to the Presbyterian Church in downtown Lexington. The service was brief; then the casket, covered with the first Confederate flag ever made, was borne to the cemetery at the south edge of town. There, the body of Thomas Jonathan Jackson was committed to the ground of the Shenandoah Valley, the Valley he loved, and his spirit was committed to his Lord and Saviour Jesus Christ. His days on earth were done, his days in heaven were just beginning.

The room where Jackson died.

XII
JACKSON MARKERS

I. First Manassas
JACKSON'S BIVOUAC
Fauquier County: U.S. 50 & 17, at Paris

Near here Jackson's men going to First Manassas sank down to rest, July 19, 1861, without placing pickets Jackson said: "Let the poor fellows sleep, I will guard the camp myself."

FIRST BATTLE OF MANASSAS
Prince William County: 4.7 miles east of Gainesville

On the Mathews Hill just to the north, the Confederates repulsed the attack of the Unionists coming from the north in the forenoon of July 21, 1861. The Union force, reinforced, drove the Confederates to the Henry Hill, just to the south. There the latter reformed under cover of Stonewall Jackson....

FIRST BATTLE OF MANASSAS
Prince William County: 4.7 miles east of Gainesville

Henry Hill lies just to the south. Here the Confederates repulsed the repeated attacks of the Union army under McDowell, July 21, 1861. Here Jackson won the name "Stonewall," and from here began McDowell's retreat that ended at Washington.

II. The Valley Campaign
JACKSON'S HEADQUARTERS
Winchester: 415 North Braddock

This house was used by Major General Thomas J. Jackson, then commanding the valley district, department of Northern Virginia, as his official headquarters from November, 1861 to March, 1862 when he left Winchester to begin his famous valley campaign.

BATTLE OF KERNSTOWN
Frederick County: 5.3 miles north of Stephens City

On the hill to the west Stonewall Jackson, late in the afternoon of March 23, 1862, attacked the Union force under Shields holding Winchester. After a fierce action, Jackson, who was greatly outnumbered, withdrew southward leaving his dead on the field. These were buried next day by the citizens of Winchester.

JACKSON'S VALLEY CAMPAIGN
Albemarle County: At Mechum's River

Near here Stonewall Jackson's troops entrained, May 4, 1862, to go west to Staunton in the move that led to the battle of McDowell, May 8, 1862.

BATTLE OF MCDOWELL
Highland County: 1 mile east of McDowell

Stonewall Jackson, to prevent a junction of Fremont and Banks, took position on the hills just to the south and beat off the attacks of Fremont's advance under Milroy, May 8, 1862. Milroy retreated that night.

BELLE BOYD AND JACKSON
Warren County: 3 miles southwest of Front Royal

Near here Stonewall Jackson was met by the spy, Belle Boyd, and informed of the position of the Union troops at Front Royal, May 24, 1862. Jackson was advancing northward attempting to get between Banks' army and Winchester.

BROTHER AGAINST BROTHER
Warren County: At Front Royal

The first Maryland Regiment, U.S.A. was a part of the force holding this town when it was attacked by Stonewall Jackson, May 23, 1862. With Jackson was the First Maryland Regiment, C.S.A. The two regiments were arrayed against each other.

CAPTURE OF FRONT ROYAL
Warren County: At Front Royal

Stonewall Jackson, moving against Banks, captured this town from a Union force under Colonel Kenly, May 23, 1862.

FIRST BATTLE OF WINCHESTER
Warren County: U.S. 522, two miles south of Nineveh

Near this spot Stonewall Jackson rested the night of May 23-24, 1862, while advancing against Banks, who occupied Winchester.

FRIST BATTLE OF WINCHESTER
Frederick County: U.S. 11 south of Winchester

On the morning of May 25, 1862, New England troops in Bank's army held this position, facing Jackson, who was advancing from the south.

FIRST BATTLE OF WINCHESTER
Frederick County: 2.3 miles north of Stephens City

The main body of Stonewall Jackson's army halted here to rest in the early morning of May 25, 1862.

FIRST BATTLE OF WINCHESTER
Frederick County: .6 mile south of Winchester

Here Stonewall Jackson in the early morning of May 25, 1862, halted his advance guard and observed the Union positions.

FIRST BATTLE OF WINCHESTER
Frederick County: S. Braddock and W. Bond Sts., Winchester

Jackson, who had pursued Banks down the valley, stormed the latter's position on the hilltops beyond the school here, May 25, 1862.

WHERE ASHBY FELL
Rockingham County: 1.3 miles south of Harrisonburg

A mile and a half east of this point, Turner Ashby, Stonewall Jackson's cavalry commander, was killed June 6, 1862, while opposing Fremont's advance.

CROSS KEYS
Rockingham County: 5 miles east of Harrisonburg

Three miles south on Mill Creek, Jackson's rear guard under Ewell was attacked by Fremont, June 8, 1862. Trimble, of Ewell's command, counter-attacked, driving the Unionists back. Jackson with the rest of his army was near Port Republic awaiting the advance of Shields up the east bank of the Shenandoah River.

PORT REPUBLIC
Rockingham County: 3 miles north of Grottoes

The cross road here roughly divides the Confederate and Union lines in the battle of June 9, 1862. Jackson attacked Shields, coming southward to join Fremont, but was repulsed. Reinforced by Ewell, Jackson attacked again and drove Shields from the field. At the same time he burned the bridge at Port Republic preventing Fremont from coming to Shields' aid.

END OF THE CAMPAIGN
At Harrisonburg

Here Stonewall Jackson, retreating up the Valley before the converging columns of Fremont and Shields turned at bay, June, 1862. A mile southeast, Jackson's cavalry commander, Ashby, was killed, June 6. At Cross Keys, six miles southeast, Ewell of Jackson's army defeated Fremont, June 8. Near Port Republic, ten miles southeast, Jackson defeated Shields, June 9. This was the end of Jackson's Valley Campaign.

JACKSON'S MARCH TO GAINES'S MILL
Hanover County: .4 mile south of Ashland

Stonewall Jackson, coming from the Shenandoah Valley, moved east over the Ashcake Road to join Lee confronting McClellan at Mechanicsville, June 26, 1862. Owing to many obstacles, Jackson did not join Lee until the next day, June 27, 1862, while the battle of Gaines's Mill was raging. His attack won the battle.

III. Seven Days' Battles
GAINES'S MILL
Hanover County: 2.7 miles south of Mechanicsville

Here Lee and Stonewall Jackson conferred in the morning of June 27, 1862. Jackson's troops halted here until A.P. Hill arrived from Beaver Dam Creek. Hill then moved southward by Gaines's Mill and Longstreet along a road near the river; Jackson turned to the east. All three columns approached the Union position on Boatswain Creek.

GAINES'S MILL
Hanover County: 1.7 miles south of Mechanicsville

Along this road Fitz-John Porter withdrew from Beaver Dam Creek in the early morning of June 27, 1862. McClellan, having learned that Stonewall Jackson was approaching Porter's rear, late at night ordered the withdrawl to another position. This was on Boatwain Creek not far from New Cold Harbor.

GAINES'S MILL
Hanover County: 5.7 miles south of Mechanicsville

Half a mile south is Boatswain Creek. The battle that was begun at Gaines's Mill by A.P. Hill, following Porter's rear guard, culminated at the Union position on Boatswain Creek. There, A.P. Hill and Longstreet moving eastward, and Jackson coming from the north converged to attack the Unionists.

GAINES'S MILL
Hanover County: 7.8 miles south of Mechanicsville

Stonewall Jackson reached this point in the afternoon of June 27, 1862, after a circuit of Gaines's Mill. When he learned that A.P. Hill and Longstreet to the west were hard pressed, he moved south to join in the attack.

GAINES'S MILL
Hanover County: 8.2 miles south of Mechanicsville

The hill to the south, part of the Union line, was assailed by Stonewall Jackson (with D.H. Hill) in the late afternoon of June 27, 1862, after A.P. Hill's and Longstreet's first assaults on the west had failed. Jackson's men carried the Union position at the bayonet point, while A.P. Hill and Longstreet were also successful.

JACKSON'S CROSSING
Madison County: 7.6 miles north of Orange

Here at Locust Dale, Stonewall Jackson's army crossed the river moving north of the battle of Cedar Mountain, August 9, 1862. The battle was fought a few hours later.

BATTLE OF CEDAR MOUNTAIN
Culpeper County: 6.1 miles south of Culpeper

Near here Jackson formed line of battle and received the attack of Banks's Corps of Pope's army. From here he attacked in turn, driving the Union forces to the northwest.

CAMPAIGN OF SECOND MANASSAS
Orange County: 3.2 miles south of Orange

Near here Stonewall Jackson camped, August 13-15, 1862, just after the Cedar Mountain engagement.

CAMPAIGN OF SECOND MANASSAS
Rappahannock County: 7.2 miles east of Massies Corner

Here Stonewall Jackson, on his march around Pope's army by the way of Jeffersonton to Bristoe Station, turned north, August 25, 1862.

CAMPAIGN OF SECOND MANASSAS
Fauquier County: At Marshall

Near here Stonewall Jackson, after a march of twenty-six miles on his way to Bristoe Station, halted for a few hours to rest his men, August 25-26, 1862.

CAMPAIGN OF SECOND MANASSAS
Fauquier County: At the Plains

Here Jackson, on his march around Pope to Bristoe Station, turned to the southeast, August 26, 1862.

CAMPAIGN OF SECOND MANASSAS
Fauquier County: U.S. 211, 4.5 miles west of Gainesville

Eight miles southeast near Bristoe, Stonewall Jackson destroyed a railroad bridge over this stream as he moved to the rear of Pope's army, August 26, 1862. Reaching Manassas, Pope's supply depot, he destroyed vast quantities of stores.

IV.
CAMPAIGN OF SECOND MANASSAS
Prince William County: Gainesville

Stonewall Jackson, moving southward on his march around Pope, was here joined by Stuart with his cavalry, August 26, 1862. From Gainesville, Jackson moved on Bristoe Station.

THOROUGHFARE GAP
Prince William County: Gainesville

Five miles northwest is Thoroughfare Gap in the Bull Run Mountains. Through this gap J.E. Johnston and Jackson came, July 19, 1861, on their way to First Manassas. Through it Lee sent Jackson, August 26, 1862, and followed with Longstreet to take part in the Second Battle of Manassas.

CAMPAIGN OF SECOND MANASSAS
Fairfax County: at Centreville

Seven miles south is Manassas, where Jackson on his turning movement around Pope destroyed vast quantitites of supplies, August 26-27, 1862. Hill and Ewell of Jackson's force, coming from Manassas, reached Centreville on their way to Jackson's position north of Groveton, August 28, 1862.

CAMPAIGN OF SECOND MANASSAS
Prince William County: 4.7 miles east of Gainesville

Here Taliaferro, of Jackson's force, came into the highway in the late night of August 26-27, 1862. He was marching from Manassas to the position about a mile and a half to the north held by Jackson in the Second Battle of Manassas.

BATTLE OF GROVETON
Prince William County: 3.5 miles east of Gainesville

Stonewall Jackson, to prevent a junction of Pope and McClellan while he was awaiting Longstreet, brought on an action here with Gibbon, August 28, 1862. Jackson's position was a short distance north of this road and facing it. Gibbon retired after a fierce fight.

V. Markers In Maryland
Frederick County

HEADQUARTERS OF LEE, JACKSON AND LONGSTREET
Route 355: South of Frederick

"Headquarters of Generals Robert E. Lee, "Stonewall" Jackson and Longstreet, September 6-9, 1862. Here was written the famous lost order, No. 191, and the proclamation to the people of Maryland.

Washington County
"STONEWALL" JACKSON'S WAY
Route 68: Southwest of Boonsboro

Under Special Orders, 191, Maj. Gen. Thomas J. Jackson led Confederate troops from Frederick to capture Harpers Ferry. On Sept. 11, 1862, Jackson's Second Corps moved from its encampment near Boonsborough to cross the Potomac at Williamsport.

VI. Fredericksburg Area
JACKSON'S MARCH TO FREDERICKSBURG
Madison County: At Madison

Stonewall Jackson, on his march from Winchester to Fredericksburg preceding the battle of Fredericksburg, camped here, November 26, 1862.

JACKSON'S HEADQUARTERS
Caroline County: 5.7 miles southeast of New Post

In an outhouse here at Moss Neck, Stonewall Jackson had his headquarters, December, 1862 - March, 1863. He was engaged in guarding the line of the Rappahannock with his corps of Lee's army.

WOUNDING OF JACKSON
Spotsylvania County: .9 miles west of Chancellorsville

Stonewall Jackson, coming from the west, surprised Howard's Corps of the Army of the Potomac, May 2, 1863. Howard retreated along this road toward Chancellorsville pursued by the Confederates. Here Jackson, in the early evening, moving in front of his line of battle to reconnoitre, fell mortally wounded by his own men.

JACKSON'S AMPUTATION
Spotsylvania County: Va. 3 east of Va. 20

Near here stood the hospital tent to which the wounded "Stonewall" Jackson was brought during the Battle of Chancellorsville. In that tent his left arm was amputated on May 3, 1863. He died seven days later at Guinea.

MUD TAVERN
Spotsylvania County: At Thornburg

Mud Tavern was the old name of this place. Six miles east at Guinea Station, Stonewall Jackson died, May 10, 1863.

BIBLIOGRAPHY

James K. Boswell,   Diary.

Bean, William G.   THE LIBERTY HALL VOLUNTEERS. Charlottesville, 1964. "STONEWALL JACKSON'S MAN": SANDIE PENDLETON. Chapel Hill, N.C., 1959.

Casler, John O.   FOUR YEARS IN THE STONEWALL BRIGADE. Marietta, Georgia. 1951.

Catton Bruce.   THE COMING FURY. New York, 1961.

Chambers, Lenoir.   STONEWALL JACKSON, New York, 1959.
Dabney, Robert L.   LIFE AND CAMPAIGNS OF LIEUTENANT GENERAL THOMAS J. JACKSON.
Douglas, Henry K.   I RODE WITH STONEWALL. Chapel Hill, 1940. New York, 1866.

Freeman, Douglas S.   LEE'S LIEUTENANTS. 3 vols. New York, 1943.
Happel, Ralph.   SALEM CHURCH EMBATTLED. 1980.
Harrison, Cary.   "Virginia Scenes in '61." In BATTLES AND LEADERS OF THE CIVIL WAR, VOL. I, New York, 1884-1887.

Jedediah Hotchkiss Papers,   the Library of Congress.

Jackson, Mary Anna.   MEMOIRS OF "STONEWALL" JACKSON. Louisville, 1895.

Kinsolving, Roberta C.   "Stonewall Jackson in Winter Quarters," THE CONFEDERATE VETERAN, VOL. XX.

Lee, Susan P.   MEMOIRS OF WILLIAM NELSON PENDLETON. Philadelphia, 1893.

Lyle, John Newton: "STONEWALL JACKSON'S GUARD." THE WASHINGTON COLLEGE COMPANY. MS in the McCormick Library, Washington and Lee University.

McDonald, Archie ed.   MAKE ME A MAP OF THE VALLEY: THE CIVIL WAR JOURNAL OF STONEWALL JACKSON'S TOPOGRAPHER. Dallas, 1973.
McDonald,   CORNELIA. A DIARY WITH REMINISCENSES OF WAR AND REFUGEE LIFE IN THE SHENANDOAH VALLEY, 1861-1865. Nashville, 1934.

McGuire, Hunter, and Christian, George.   THE CONFEDERATE CAUSE AND CONDUCT IN THE WAR BETWEEN THE STATES. Richmond, 1907.

Poague, William.   GUNNER WITH STONEWALL. Jackson, Tenn., 1957.

Robertson, James I.   THE STONEWALL BRIGADE. Baton Rouge, 1963.

Smith, James P.   "With Stonewall Jackson," SOUTHERN HISTORICAL
                             SOCIETY PAPERS. VOL. 5. RICHMOND, 1920.

Tanner, Robert G.   STONEWALL IN THE VALLEY. New York, 1976.

U.S. War Department,   WAR OF THE REBELLION: A COMPILATION OF
comp.   THE OFFICIAL RECORDS OF THE UNION AND
                             CONFEDERATE ARMIES. 128 vols. Washington,
                             1880-1901.

Vandiver, Frank.   MIGHTY STONEWALL. New York, 1957.

NOTES
I
THE MAN

1. The Virginia Military Institute, often called "the West Point of the South," was founded in 1839. One of the founders was Colonel John T.L. Preston. He wanted the school to be related to the State, to the Military, and to be an institute rather than a college. General George S. Patton and General George C. Marshall of World War II fame had military roots at V.M.I.

2. Hunter Holmes McGuire was the son of a prominent Winchester family. During the war he became Surgeon of First Brigade, Army of the Shenandoah. He was very close to Jackson, performing surgery on the General's arm, and later going with the body to Lexington for funeral services. After the war he became very prominent in Richmond, founding St. Luke's hospital, teaching surgery, and giving medical and military addresses. He was elected President of the American Medical Association.

3. For biographical material on the early years of Jackson, see Frank Vandiver's MIGHTY STONEWALL, New York, 1957 and Lenoir Chambers, New York, 1959.

4. Jackson came to West Point as an awkward, poorly educated country bumpkin. He studied hard and graduated in 1846, ranking 17th in a class of fifty-nine cadets.

5. Jackson won two brevets during the Mexican War. He served with the First Artillery.

6. Dr. George Junkin was born near New Cumberland, Pennsylvania. He became a minister and educator. After serving as President of Lafayette College in Easton, he was called to the presidency of Washington College in Lexington, Virginia. It was here that his daughter Eleanor met Thomas J. Jackson and later married him. Tom made his home with the Junkin's for awhile, and like his father-in-law, was devestated with the early death of Ellie. During the rest of his life Jackson remained a close friend of Ellie's sister, Margaret Junkin Preston.

7. Colonel Preston went with the corps of cadets from Lexington to Harpers Ferry and Charles Town for the hanging of John Brown. His description of the events is most graphic.

8. Jackson's nervous and shy personality is mentioned numerous times in a collection of Hill's letters contained in the Dabney materials at the University of Texas. These letters are perhaps the most revealing of Jackson's life in Lexington.

9. See Robert L. Dabney THE LIFE OF GENERAL STONEWALL JACKSON New York, 1866. This was the first biography of Jackson.

II
SPARKS

1. For more information about the causes of the war and the political rhetoric see Bruce Catton, THE COMING FURY, New York, 1961.

2. John D. Imboden, "Jackson at Harpers Ferry in 1861," "in BATTLES and LEADERS OF THE CIVIL WAR," New York, 1887. Vol. I, pp. 112-121.

3. Cornelia McDonald, A DIARY with REMINISCENCES OF WAR AND REFUGEE LIFE IN THE SHENANDOAH VALLEY. 1860-1865. Nashville, 1934, pp. 14-15. Constance and Cary Harrison, "Virginia Scenes in '61," in B and L, Vol. I, p. 160.

4. For a chronology of Jackson's military life, see Henry K. Douglas, I RODE WITH STONEWALL, Chapel Hill, 1940; the Pendleton Papers, the University of North Carolina; and the Jedediah Hotchkiss Papers and Diary, the Library of Congress. From March 1862 to the death of Jackson. Jed's record is a must for anyone interested in the man they called "Stonewall."

5. Dr. William White left the Charlottesville area and came to Lexington at the age of forty-eight. He became pastor of the Presbyterian Church and Jackson's friend and teacher. Jackson looked upon him as his spiritual commander. Several sons became members of the Liberty Hall Volunteers, the college company that became part of Jackson's command. Son Hugh fell at the battle of Second Manassas. Dr. White also conducted Jackson's funeral service. The cleric is buried in the same cemetery with Jackson.

6. Mary Anna Jackson, MEMOIRS OF STONEWALL JACKSON. Louisville, 1898. A must for any Jackson reader.

7. Jackson to his wife, April 22, 1861.

8. Jackson to his wife, April 28, 1861.

9. Col. Preston served on Jackson's staff for awhile, and then returned to duties at V.M.I. He served on the faculty and the Board of Visitors for many years, and wrote one of the first histories of his beloved Institute.

10. Imboden in B and L, Vol. I, pp. 121-125.

11. Ibid., p. 121.

12. Mr. Barbour served at the armory in Harpers Ferry and later in Confederate service. He died young.

13. Jackson was quick to note the strategic importance of the Shenandoah Valley. In a note to Lee on May 21, 1861, he stated, "I would suggest that a force destined for the northwest be assembled for the defense of this part of the State at Winchester."

14. For more reading about Jackson's first command, see James I. Robertson's, THE STONEWALL BRIGADE, Baton Rouge, 1963.

15. Jackson to his wife, June 4, 1861.

16. Douglas S. Freeman, LEE'S LIEUTENANTS, New York, 1943. Three vols.

17. For additional material on Alexander Swift Pendleton see Bean, William, "Sandie Pendleton, Stonewall Jackson's Man," Chapel Hill, 1959, and Susan P. Lee ed. MEMOIRS OF WILLIAM NELSON PENDLETON. Philadelphia, 1893.

18. Douglas, p. 6.

John W. Schildt

19. Jackson to his wife, June 16, 1861.

20. W.G. Bean, THE LIBERTY HALL VOLUNTEERS, Charlottesville, 1964. The letters and notes from members of the unit describe life at Camp Stevens.

21. Edwin (Ned) Lee, was a distant relative of Robert E. Lee. A graduate of William and Mary College, he practiced law, and married Susan Pendleton, Sandie's sister. He was a member of the 33rd Virginia until forced to resign by ill health.

22. OFFICIAL RECORDS, WAR OF THE REBELLION, I, ii, p. 185 cited hereafter as O.R., Mrs. Jackson, p. 166.

23. Mrs. Jackson, p. 166.

24. Jackson to his wife, July 4, 1861.

25. Jackson to his wife, July 16, 1861.

III
"A STONEWALL"

1. John O. Casler, FOUR YEARS IN THE STONEWALL BRIGADE. Marietta, Ga. 1951. p. 21.

2. John Newton Lyle, "Stonewall Jackson's Guard, The Washington College Company." MS in the McCormick Library. Washington and Lee University, p. 77.

3. The "Lone Sentenial Marker" is located at Paris, Virginia. The writer was James Ryder Randall.

4. For more information on the name "Stonewall" see Freeman, LEE'S Lieutenants. Vol. I, p. 82 and Vandiver. p. 161.

5. There is little material available on the late summer and early autumn of 1861. Jackson was apparently very busy with training and administrative duties.

6. Jackson to his wife, September 30, 1861.

7. Mrs. Jackson, pp. 198-199.

8. This speech is recorded in all the major Jackson books. However, Douglas says he recorded it as he remembered it. See Douglas pp. 16-17, and his notes on pp. 361-362.

IV
WINCHESTER

1. Vandiver, p. 414. Winchester was like a second home to Jackson. He loved the residents and they loved him.

2. Jackson to his wife, November 16, 1861.

3. Rev. William Graham, pastor of the Kent Street Presbyterian Church, was born in New York, attended Princeton, served in Winchester for half a century and was Jackson's friend.

4. Richard Garnett commanded the Stonewall Brigade for four months. He invoked Jackson's anger at Kernstown. He was killed at Gettysburg.

5. The Chesapeake and Ohio Canal runs from Washington, D.C. to Cumberland, Maryland, approximately 185 miles in length. The canal along with the Baltimore and Ohio Railroad was a vital source of supply and transportation. Throughout the war the Confederates made repeated efforts to disrupt traffic on the canal.

6. Robert Poague, GUNNER WITH STONEWALL, Jackson, Tennessee. 1957. p. 12.

7. The Romney Expedition was begun on January 1, 1863. Jackson's goal was to drive the Yankee forces from the area and protect Virginia from invasion. However, the weather and supply factors made the invasion and expedition a disaster. It caused much suffering and almost caused a mutiny among some of the troops. It caused some of his officers to go over his head in complaining to officials in Richmond.

8. Rev. Graham, quoted in Mrs. Jackson, p. 212.

9. Jackson's resignation is discussed in THE OFFICIAL RECORDS, WAR OF THE REBELLION, I, v, 1.040-1,041, 1,046, 1,053, 1,062-1,063.

10. Poague, 18.

11. Robert G. Tanner. STONEWALL IN THE VALLEY. New York, 1976. p. 82.

12. O.R. I, v, 1,053.

13. Mrs. Jackson, p. 215.

14. Ibid.

15. Alexander Robison Boteler was born in Shepherdstown on May 16, 1815. Graudating from Princeton, he enetered politics and was elected to Congress in 1858. In the early days of the war he was elected to the Confederate Congress from the Winchester District.

16. Diary of James Keith Boswell, February 25, 1862.

17. Nathaniel P. Banks served the State of Massachusetts in Congress before and after the war. He was also Governor. In 1862 he opposed Jackson as head of the Union Dept. of the Shenandoah.

V
THE VALLEY CAMPAIGN

1. Strasburg was an important rail center, being the western terminus of the Manassas Gap Railroad.

2. Mount Jackson, forty-two miles south of Winchester, was selected by General Jackson as his base of supply upon the evacuation of Winchester. From this town he started north again to confront the Yankees at Kernstown near the end of March.

3. Robert L. Dabney, THE LIFE AND CAMPAIGNS OF LIEUTENANT GENERAL THOMAS J. JACKSON, New York, 1886. p. 314.

4. Vandiver, pp. 208-209.

5. Ibid. p. 217.

6. Jed Hotchkiss was born in New York, came to Virginia on a visit and was so impressed he decided to stay. He opened several academies and taught. He also studied engineering and mapping. Entering Confederate service, he became Jackson's map maker. His notes and correspondence with other staff members have served all Jackson scholars. After the war he lived in Staunton.

7. Jackson's letter, April 16, 1862.

8. Hotchkiss Journal, April 13, 1862.

9. R.L. Dabney was another Presbyterian cleric who became a friend of Jackson. He was a seminary professor at Union when he became a member of Jackson's staff. His biology of Jackson appeared in 1866. After the war he taught at the University of Texas. He died on January 3, 1898.

10. Richard L. Taylor, the only son of Zachary Taylor, was born at Springfield near Louisville, Ky., on January 2, 1879. Graduating from Yale, he managed a sugar plantation in St. Charles Parish, Louisiana. After service with Jackson he held an independent command in the southwest. He writes of his service with Jackson in DESTRUCTION AND RESURRECTION. New York, 1879.

11. Douglas, p. 59.

12. Idem.

13. GENERAL ORDER, Number 53, May 26, 1862, published after the great victory at Winchester.

14. At Winchester, Hunter McGuire recommended freeing captured Union doctors. Some scholars feel this was a forerunner of the Red Cross.

15. Major J. Welles Hawks like Hotchkiss came from the north and settled in Charles Town. He became a leading citizen. And when war broke out joined the ranks of the Second Virginia.

16. Douglas, p. 75.

17. Freeman, Vol. 2, pp. 432.

18. O.R. I xii, pt. 1, p. 712.

19. Imboden, "Jackson in the Shenandoah." BATTLES AND LEADERS, Vol. II. p. 293.

20. Cross Keys is a group of homes in rural Rockingham County along Route 276. Once there was a village and a "Cross Keys Tavern."

21. Jackson was convinced that when the troops took a break, they should stretch out. He made the remark about resting all over when lying down, on several occasions.

VI
THE SUMMER OF 1862

1. Jackson has been greatly criticized for his failures during the Seven Days Campaign. However, he was suffering from fatigue and he was not familiar with the area. Other commanders had been there a week or more and they still became lost. There were many lost opportunities for the Confederate cause during this week.

2. Dr. Moses Hoge ministered to Confederate troops and government officials at this time and throughout the war. He and Jackson had mutual respect for each other.

3. Dr. Daniel Ewing was yet another Presbyterian clergyman with which Jackson conversed.

4. John Neff was from a peace-loving Dunkard family. He rose to the Command of the Thirty-third Virginia and fell upon the field of battle at Second Manassas.

VII

1. Lee states his reasons for the invasion of Maryland in O.R. I, XIX. Pt. II, p. 590. They are to raise the morale of the South; to cause the invader, the North, to leave Virginia soil; and to give the farmers an opportunity to harvest their crops.

2. Hotchkiss diary, September 4 and 5, 1862.

3. Douglas, p. 150.

4. Ibid. p. 152.

5. The Bower was the Dandridge home, a large estate along the Opequon Creek. Here the Confederate cavalry made camp in the autumn of 1862. Troopers rode to Jackson's HQ's at Bunker Hill.

VIII

1. Cornelia McDonald described the General in church on November 16, 1862.

2. Mrs. Jackson, p. 509.

3. Ibid., pp. 360-361.

4. Smith, p. 25.

5. See also Ralph Happel, SALEM CHURCH Embattled, 1980.

IX

1. Hamilton's Crossing is roughly three and a half miles southeast of Fredericksburg. Today it is near the end of the National Park road that runs along the lines of the Confederate defense.

2. Jackson to his wife, December 16, 1862.

3. Moss Neck has be a favorite for the Jackson reader. Here Jackson made his headquarters from December 16, 1862, until March 16, 1863. Here he caught up on administrative detail, met with visitors and officers from other commands. Jackson also watched his beloved Sandie Pendleton fall in love with Kate Corbin. And while at Moss Neck, Jackson cut out paper dolls with Janie Corbin. The estate is ten miles south of Fredericksburg. The house was built in 1856.

4. For a very moving description of Moss Neck see Roberta C. Kinsolving, "Stonewall Jackson in Winter Quarters," THE CONFEDERATE VETERAN. VOL. XX. See also Douglas, 207-215, Smith, pp. 35-39.

5. Douglas, p. 208 and Smith p. 38.

6. Bean, p. 103. Pendleton sets forth his feelings in a letter to Mary.

7. Jackson, letter to Boteler.

X
THE WINTER OF 1863

1. Boswell, Diary.

2. Jackson, letter, January 6, 1863.

3. Charles J. Faulkner was fifty-five years of age and had been Ambassador to France.

4. Jackson, letter, January 17, 1863.

5. Jackson, letter, February 3, 1863.

6. Moses D. Hoge came from a long line of distinguished Presbyterian pastors. He was to serve the Second Presbyterian Church of Richmond for nearly fifty years. In the fall of 1862 he went to Europe seeking Bibles and religious tracts for the Confederate soldiers. He had a close escape running the blockade. Jackson's wife was with Mrs. Hoge when she received the news of her husband's wounding. Mrs. Hoge was with Mrs. Jackson the night Stonewall died. Dr. Hoge was crushed by the fall of the Confederacy. In fact, he fled the city of Richmond with many of the government leaders. He knew them well, for they oftern worshipped at Second Presbyterian Church. He experienced depression over the Union occupation. Hoge was in great demand as a speaker in the south. He became very good friends with Dr. Hunter McGuuire. The two men sailed to Europe on several occasions.

7. The Boswell Diary.

8. Ibid, March 17, 1863.

9. "The Gallant" John Pelham commanded Stuart's Horse Artillery. He was killed in a minor clash near Kelly's Ford. Some felt this was an omen of thing to come for the Confederacy.

10. From information supplied by Robert Krick, noted Jackson authority and chief historian at Fredericksburg.

11. Hotchkiss Journal, April 11, 1863.

12. Mrs. Jackson, p. 407.

13. Ibid., p. 409.

14. Mrs. Jackson, pp. 410-411. "With Stonewall Jackson."

15. See Mrs. Jackson, 410-415 for more information.

16. Mrs. Jackson, p. 412.

17. Ibid, p. 415, and Smith, p. 44.

XI
THEN COMETH THE END

1. Smith, p. 45.

2. Ibid, p. 46.

3. Ibid, pp. 50-51.

4. For more on the wounding of Jackson see Hunter McGuire. "Account of the Wounding and Death of Stonewall Jackson," Hunter McGuire and George Christian, THE CONFEDERATE CAUSE AND CONDUCT IN THE WAR BETWEEN THE STATES, Richmond, 1907. pp. 219-229. Smith, pp. 51-54.

5. McGuire, p. 224.

6. McGuire account.

7. Idem., and Dabney, pp. 712-713.

8. McGuire, p. 226.

9. Mrs. Jackson, pp. 453-457. McGuire, 227-228.

10. Idem. and Freeman, II, pp. 669-682.

11. Major Sandie Pendleton to Governor Letcher, May 10, 1863. The Pendleton Papers.

12. Douglas, p. 229.